I0012411

TypeScript for Backend Development

Backend applications with Node.js, Express, and modern frameworks

Adriam Miller

Discover Other Books in the Series

"TypeScript for Beginners: A Beginner's Guide to the Future of JavaScript"

"TypeScript for Blockchain: Unlock the full potential of TypeScript in Web3 development"

"TypeScript for DevOps: The Secret Weapon for Automating, Scaling, and Securing Your Infrastructure"

"Typescript for Front End Development: Reduce Errors, Boost Productivity, and Master Modern Web Development Like a Pro"

"TypeScript for JavaScript Developers: The Essential Guide for JavaScript Developers to Write Safer, Scalable, and More Efficient Code"

"Typescript for Microservices: Learn How to Leverage TypeScript to Develop Robust, Maintainable, and Efficient Microservices Architecture"

"TypeScript for Mobile Application Development: Build Faster, Safer, and Smarter Applications with Ease"

"TypeScript for Web Development: Boost Your Productivity, Eliminate Costly Errors, and Build Scalable Web Applications with TypeScript"

Copyright © 2024 by Adriam Miller.

All rights reserved. No part of this book may be used or reproduced in any form whatsoever without written permission except in the case of brief quotations in critical articles or reviews.

Printed in the United States of America.

For more information, or to book an event, contact :
(Email & Website)

Book design by Adriam Miller
Cover design by Adriam Miller

Disclaimer

The information provided in this book, **"TypeScript for Backend Development: backend applications with Node.js, Express, and modern framework"** by Adrian Miller, is for **educational and informational purposes only**. The content is designed to help readers understand TypeScript programming.

Introduction

Welcome to "**TypeScript for Backend Development: Building Backend Applications with Node.js**, Express, and Modern Frameworks"! In today's digital landscape, the ability to develop robust and scalable web applications is essential, making a deep understanding of backend development increasingly important. This eBook is designed to assist you in utilizing TypeScript to create powerful backend applications, with a focus on the widely-used frameworks of Node.js and Express.

As the need for web applications grows, developers are in constant pursuit of tools and technologies that enhance productivity while also elevating the quality and maintainability of their code. TypeScript, a typed superset of JavaScript, offers static typing and various features that facilitate early error detection, leading to cleaner and more resilient applications.

In this Book, we will undertake a thorough exploration of the core principles of TypeScript and its effective application in backend development. You will learn how to configure your development environment, build RESTful APIs using Express, manage databases, and adopt contemporary best practices to create maintainable applications. We will cover key topics such as:

Setting Up Your TypeScript Environment: Learn how to configure your development environment for TypeScript, including essential tools and libraries.

Understanding TypeScript Basics: Dive into the core features of TypeScript, including types, interfaces, and modules, which will help you write more robust code.

Building RESTful APIs with Express: Step-by-step instructions on creating RESTful APIs using Express.js, along with practical examples.

Database Connectivity: Explore how to connect your applications with databases, including SQL and NoSQL options, and manage data effectively.

Implementing Modern Frameworks: Learn about popular frameworks and libraries that complement TypeScript and enhance productivity, such as NestJS.

Whether you are a beginner embarking on your programming journey, or an experienced developer looking to explore TypeScript for backend development, this eBook will provide you with the knowledge and skills necessary to thrive in today's dynamic tech landscape.

By the end of this book, you will not only possess a strong understanding of TypeScript and its applications in backend development but also the confidence to tackle real-world projects and challenges. Let's dive in together and unlock the full potential of TypeScript in creating scalable, high-quality backend solutions!

Chapter 1: Introduction to TypeScript for Backend Development

The inherent flexibility and dynamism of JavaScript have facilitated swift advancements; however, the absence of static typing has frequently resulted in difficulties, particularly within larger codebases. This is where TypeScript becomes relevant. TypeScript, a superset of JavaScript created by Microsoft, introduces optional static typing to the language, enabling developers to identify errors during compile time instead of runtime, thereby enhancing overall code maintainability.

1.1 What is TypeScript?

TypeScript is an open-source programming language that extends JavaScript by incorporating static type definitions. The main objectives of TypeScript are to improve the development experience and bolster the reliability of JavaScript applications. By integrating types, interfaces, and generics, TypeScript equips developers with the means to produce clearer and more predictable code. TypeScript code is transpiled into standard JavaScript, which can be executed in any environment that supports JavaScript, including web browsers and server-side platforms like Node.js. Consequently, TypeScript can effortlessly integrate with existing JavaScript libraries and frameworks, making it a flexible option for developers aiming to enhance their JavaScript applications.

1.2 Why Use TypeScript for Backend Development?

Type Safety: One of the most significant advantages of TypeScript is its static typing system. By defining types, developers can catch errors early in the development process. This is particularly beneficial in a backend context where the data structure can be complex and require precise handling.

Improved Code Quality: TypeScript encourages better coding practices through the use of interfaces and type annotations. This leads to more maintainable code and easier refactorings. Developers can clearly define the shape of data being handled, making it easier to understand and work with.

Enhanced IDE Support: Modern IDEs and text editors have excellent support for TypeScript, providing features such as autocompletion, type checking, and inline documentation. This increases developer productivity and reduces the learning curve for new team members.

Interoperability with JavaScript: Since TypeScript is a superset of JavaScript, developers can gradually adopt it in existing JavaScript projects. This makes it easier to transition to TypeScript without the need for a complete rewrite. Teams can start leveraging TypeScript's benefits for new modules or features while continuing to support legacy JavaScript code.

Strong Community and Ecosystem: TypeScript has a thriving community that contributes numerous third-party libraries, frameworks, and tools. Popular frameworks such as NestJS and Express have good support for TypeScript, providing extensive type definitions and making it easier for developers to build scalable applications.

1.3 Getting Started with TypeScript

To start developing with TypeScript in a backend environment, you'll need to set up a few essential tools:

Node.js: Since most backend development with TypeScript is done using Node.js, ensuring you have the latest version installed is crucial.

TypeScript Compiler: You can install TypeScript globally using npm:

```bash
npm install -g typescript
```

Development Environment: Choose an Integrated Development Environment (IDE) that provides excellent TypeScript support. Popular choices include Visual Studio Code, WebStorm, and Atom.

Package Management: Familiarize yourself with package management tools like npm or yarn to manage dependencies for your TypeScript application.

Basic TypeScript Configuration: Create a configuration file (`tsconfig.json`) for TypeScript. This file allows you to customize the compiler settings, such as target version, module type, and strictness settings.

```json
{
"compilerOptions": { "target": "es6", "module": "commonjs", "strict": true, "esModuleInterop": true, "skipLibCheck": true,
"forceConsistentCasingInFileNames": true
```

```
}

}

` ` `
```

In the following chapters, we will dive deeper into TypeScript's features, exploring its type system, and how to leverage it effectively in a backend development context. We'll cover key topics such as setting up a TypeScript project with Node.js, using popular frameworks like Express and NestJS, and best practices for organizing your code.

The Power of TypeScript for Backend

In this chapter, we'll explore the power of TypeScript for backend applications, its unique features, and how it can elevate the development experience while enhancing code quality and team collaboration.

1. Understanding TypeScript

TypeScript, developed by Microsoft, is a superset of JavaScript that introduces static typing to the JavaScript ecosystem. This means that developers can define types for variables, function parameters, return values, and more, allowing for greater control over the code and reducing the likelihood of runtime errors.

1.1 The Benefits of Static Typing

One of the core advantages of TypeScript is its static typing. This feature helps catch type-related errors at compile time rather than at runtime, providing a safety net that can lead to fewer bugs in production code. For instance, if a function is defined to accept a parameter of type `number`, TypeScript will throw an error at compile time if a string is mistakenly passed to it. This leads to more predictable behavior of code and a smoother development experience.

2. Improved Developer Experience ### 2.1 Autocompletion and IntelliSense

TypeScript offers robust tooling support that enhances developer productivity. Integrated development environments (IDEs) such as Visual Studio Code and WebStorm leverage TypeScript's type information to provide autocompletion and IntelliSense features. These tools help developers write code faster and with more confidence, as they can quickly access documentation and possible properties or methods as they code.

2.2 Easier Refactoring

Refactoring is a necessary part of maintaining high-quality code, especially in large applications. TypeScript's static typing system enhances the safety and ease of refactoring code. When a type is changed, TypeScript can track all usages and highlight where adjustments are needed, making it simpler and safer to modify code across an extensive codebase.

3. Enhanced Maintainability and Readability ### 3.1 Explicit Interfaces and Type Definitions

TypeScript encourages the use of explicit interfaces and types. When creating APIs for backend services, defining clear interfaces for data models and response structures makes the code more understandable. Team members can quickly grasp the expected data shapes and methods, leading to improved collaboration and reduced onboarding time for new developers.

3.2 Modular Code Structure

TypeScript's support for modules and namespaces allows for a modular approach to development. By organizing code in smaller, reusable components, teams can develop and maintain applications more efficiently. This modularity aligns well with modern software architecture practices such as microservices and serverless frameworks, which emphasize small, independently deployable units.

4. Compatibility with JavaScript Ecosystem ### 4.1 Leveraging Existing JavaScript Libraries

One of TypeScript's strongest aspects is its seamless integration with the existing JavaScript ecosystem. Developers can easily leverage popular JavaScript libraries and frameworks, such as Express, NestJS, and more, without any compatibility issues. TypeScript provides type definitions for many libraries through DefinitelyTyped, enabling developers to work with powerful tools while enjoying the benefits of static typing.

4.2 Gradual Adoption

For teams already invested in JavaScript, TypeScript offers a gradual adoption path. It's possible to start using TypeScript in existing JavaScript projects by renaming `.js` files to `.ts` and incrementally introducing types. This flexibility allows teams to experience the benefits of TypeScript without needing to rewrite their entire codebase at once.

5. Scalability and Performance

5.1 Building Scalable Applications

As applications grow, scalability becomes a crucial concern. TypeScript's strong typing helps manage complex code structures and large codebases, making it easier to reason about the application's behavior. Developers can structure their backend logic with confidence, ensuring that new features and updates do not introduce regressions.

5.2 Performance Considerations

TypeScript compiles down to plain JavaScript, and thus inherits JavaScript's performance capabilities. With TypeScript, developers can leverage modern JavaScript features while maintaining compatibility with older environments. Furthermore, the compile-time checks can produce optimized JavaScript code, enhancing performance at runtime.

TypeScript has proven itself to be a powerful ally for backend developers. Its static typing, enhanced developer experience, improved maintainability, compatibility with the JavaScript ecosystem, and scalability features represent a significant evolution in how we approach backend development. As organizations continue to seek efficient, reliable, and maintainable solutions, TypeScript stands out as a robust choice that meets modern development demands.

Setting Up Your TypeScript Development Environment

This chapter walks you through the steps to set up your TypeScript development environment, whether you are a beginner or someone looking to transition from JavaScript to TypeScript.

1. Prerequisites

Before diving into TypeScript, ensure you have the following prerequisites installed on your machine:

- **Node.js and npm:** Node.js is a JavaScript runtime that enables you to run JavaScript outside the browser. npm (Node Package Manager) comes with Node.js and allows you to install packages easily. To check if you have Node.js and npm installed, run the following commands in your terminal:

```bash
node -v npm -v
```

If these commands return version numbers, you're all set. If not, download and install Node.js from the [official website](https://nodejs.org/).

A Text Editor or IDE: Choose a text editor or Integrated Development Environment (IDE) that supports TypeScript development. Popular options include:

Visual Studio Code (VSCode): A highly recommended and widely-used editor with TypeScript support.

WebStorm: A powerful IDE developed by JetBrains, often preferred for TypeScript projects.

16

Atom, Sublime Text, or Vim: Other editors with plugin support for TypeScript. ## 2. Installing TypeScript

Once you have Node.js and npm installed, installing TypeScript is straightforward. You can install TypeScript globally using npm, which allows you to use the `tsc` (TypeScript Compiler) command from any terminal window. To install TypeScript globally, run:

```bash

npm install -g typescript
```

To check if the installation was successful, verify the TypeScript version:

```bash tsc -v
```

If it returns the version number, you're ready to start using TypeScript! ## 3. Setting Up a New TypeScript Project

Now that TypeScript is installed, let's set up a new project. Create a new directory for your project:

```bash

mkdir my-typescript-project cd my-typescript-project
```

Next, initialize a new npm project. This will create a `package.json` file, where you can manage your project dependencies and scripts:

```bash
npm init -y
```

After initializing the npm project, install TypeScript as a development dependency:

```bash
npm install --save-dev typescript
```

3.1. Creating a TypeScript Configuration File

TypeScript uses a configuration file called `tsconfig.json` to define compiler options and working directories. You can create this file manually or by using the TypeScript CLI. To create a `tsconfig.json` using the CLI, run:

```bash
npx tsc --init
```

This command generates a default `tsconfig.json` file. You can customize it according to your project needs. Here's a brief explanation of some commonly used options:

compilerOptions.target: Specifies the ECMAScript target version. For instance, setting it to "ES6" to compile down to ES6.

compilerOptions.module: Defines the module system (e.g., "commonjs", "es6").

compilerOptions.outDir: The directory where compiled JavaScript files will be placed.

include: An array of files or directories to include in

the compilation.

exclude: Files or directories to exclude from the compilation. Here's an example of a simple `tsconfig.json`:

```json
{

"compilerOptions": { "target": "ES6", "module": "commonjs", "outDir": "./dist", "strict": true, "esModuleInterop": true

},

"include": ["src/**/*"], "exclude": ["node_modules"]

}
```

4. Writing Your First TypeScript Code

Create a new folder named `src` within your project directory to store your TypeScript files:

```bash
mkdir src
```

Inside the `src` folder, create a file named `index.ts`:

```typescript
// src/index.ts
const greet = (name: string): string => { return `Hello, ${name}!`;
};
console.log(greet("TypeScript"));
```

```
```

This simple TypeScript code defines a function that greets a user by name. ## 5. Compiling TypeScript

To compile your TypeScript code into JavaScript, run the TypeScript compiler from the terminal:

```bash npx tsc
```

This command will use the settings from `tsconfig.json` to compile any TypeScript `.ts` files in the `src` directory and output them to the `dist` folder (as specified by the `outDir` option).

6. Running Your Compiled Code

Once compiled, you can run your JavaScript code using Node.js. Navigate to the `dist` folder and run the

`index.js` file:

```bash
node dist/index.js
```

If everything is set up correctly, you should see the output:
```

Hello, TypeScript!
```

7. Adding TypeScript to Your Workflow

With TypeScript set up and your first project created, you might consider streamlining your development process:

Watch Mode: To automatically compile TypeScript files when they change, use the watch mode:

```bash
npx tsc --watch
```

ESLint and Prettier: Add ESLint for linting and Prettier for code formatting to maintain code quality. You can install them using npm:

```bash
npm install --save-dev eslint prettier eslint-plugin-prettier eslint-config-prettier
```

Scripts in package.json: Define scripts in your `package.json` for easier command execution. Here's an example:

```json
"scripts": { "build": "tsc",
"start": "node dist/index.js", "watch": "tsc --watch"
}
```

Now you can run `npm run build`, `npm start`, or `npm run watch` to compile, run, or watch your TypeScript files, respectively.

Setting up your TypeScript development environment is a straightforward process that lays the foundation for efficient and error-free development. In this chapter, we

21

covered the prerequisites, installation process, project setup, writing your first TypeScript code, and tips for integrating TypeScript into your workflow. With this foundation, you are now ready to explore more complex TypeScript functionalities and build robust applications.

Chapter 2: TypeScript Fundamentals for Backend Developers

TypeScript, a statically-typed superset of JavaScript, is becoming an essential tool for backend developers looking to leverage the power of typed programming in their Node.js applications. This chapter will introduce you to the fundamental concepts of TypeScript tailored specifically for backend development.

2.1 Understanding TypeScript

TypeScript is developed and maintained by Microsoft and is designed to enhance JavaScript by providing optional static typing, interfaces, and other features commonly found in strongly typed languages. One of the key advantages of using TypeScript is its ability to catch errors at compile time rather than at runtime, leading to fewer bugs and more reliable code.

Key Features of TypeScript:

Static Typing: Allows you to specify variable types, function return types, and object shapes. This helps in reducing bugs and improves code clarity.

Interfaces and Types: You can define complex data structures using `interface` and `type`, ensuring your objects conform to specific contracts.

Type Inference: TypeScript can often infer types based on the context, making the transition from JavaScript seamless while still providing type safety.

Advanced Object-Oriented Programming: TypeScript supports modern JavaScript features, including classes, inheritance, and access modifiers, allowing you to adopt object-oriented principles easily.

ES6+ Features: TypeScript allows you to utilize the latest JavaScript features, including async/await, destructuring, and modules, ensuring your code remains modern and maintainable.

2.2 Setting Up TypeScript in Your Backend Project

To start using TypeScript in your Node.js project, you need to set up your environment. Follow these steps:

Install Node.js: Ensure you have Node.js installed. You can download it from nodejs.org.

Initialize Your Project:

```bash
mkdir my-backend-project cd my-backend-project npm init -y
```

Install TypeScript:

```bash
npm install --save-dev typescript
```

Create tsconfig.json: This file holds the configuration required for TypeScript. You can create it using the following command:

```bash
npx tsc --init
```

Configure tsconfig.json: Here's a basic setup:

```json
{
"compilerOptions": { "target": "ES6", "module":
"commonjs", "rootDir": "./src",

"outDir": "./dist", "strict": true, "esModuleInterop": true

},
"include": ["src/**/*"],

"exclude": ["node_modules", "**/*.spec.ts"]

}
```

Directory Structure: Organize your project as follows:

```
/my-backend-project src

index.ts        # Your entry point

dist     # Compiled JavaScript code package.json

tsconfig.json
```

2.3 Basic TypeScript Constructs ### 2.3.1 Types

TypeScript provides several built-in types. Here are a few fundamental ones:

- **Primitive Types**:

```typescript
const name: string = "John Doe"; const age: number = 30;
```

```typescript
const isActive: boolean = true;
```

- **Array Types**:
```typescript
const scores: number[] = [100, 95, 80];
const names: Array<string> = ["Alice", "Bob"];
```

- **Tuple Types**:
```typescript
const user: [string, number] = ["Alice", 25];
```

- **Enum Types**:
```typescript
enum Role { Admin, User, Guest
}
const currentUserRole: Role = Role.Admin;
```

2.3.2 Functions

TypeScript allows you to define function parameters and return types explicitly. This enhances readability and prevents unintended behaviors.

```typescript
function greet(name: string): string { return `Hello,
${name}`;
```

```
}
const greeting: string = greet("Alice");
```

2.3.3 Interfaces

Interfaces in TypeScript allow you to define the shape of an object, which is crucial in backend development as you often deal with complex data structures.

```typescript
interface User { id: number; name: string; email: string;

isActive: boolean;

}

function registerUser(user: User): void {

// Logic to register the user

}
```

2.4 Integrating TypeScript with Node.js

TypeScript works seamlessly with Node.js, making it easy to build server-side applications. You can use popular frameworks like Express.js or newer options like NestJS with TypeScript to build robust servers.

Example: Setting Up an Express Server

Install Express and Type Definitions:

```bash
npm install express

npm install --save-dev @types/express
```

```
```

Create a Simple Server (`src/server.ts`):

```typescript
import express, { Request, Response } from 'express';
const app = express(); const port = 3000;
app.get('/', (req: Request, res: Response) => {
res.send('Hello TypeScript with Express!');
});
app.listen(port, () => {
console.log(`Server running at http://localhost:${port}`);
});
```

Compile and Run:

```bash
bash npx tsc
node dist/server.js
```

2.5 Best Practices for TypeScript in Backend Development

Leverage Type Safety: Always define types for function parameters and return values to ensure that your functions behave as expected.

Utilize Interfaces and Types: Make use of interfaces to define complex objects. This promotes consistency across your codebase.

Enable Strict Mode: In `tsconfig.json`, set `"strict":

true` to enable all strict type-checking options.

Keep Your Code Modular: Organize your code into modules and use ES6 imports/exports to maintain clear separation of concerns.

Write Unit Tests: Incorporate testing frameworks like Jest or Mocha, and write tests in TypeScript to ensure code quality.

TypeScript brings a wealth of benefits for backend developers. Its static typing, clear syntax, and modern features make it a powerful choice for creating scalable and maintainable applications.

Understanding TypeScript Types, Interfaces, and Enums

This allows developers to catch errors at compile time rather than runtime, improving code quality and maintainability. In this chapter, we will explore three foundational features of TypeScript: types, interfaces, and enums. Understanding these concepts is crucial to harnessing the full potential of TypeScript in your projects.

1. Types

Types are the core building blocks of TypeScript. They define the shape and behavior of data structures, providing a way to specify what kinds of values can be assigned to variables. TypeScript offers a variety of built-in types, as well as the ability to define custom types.

1.1. Built-in Types

Here are some of the most commonly used built-in types in TypeScript:

- **Number**: Represents both integer and floating-point numbers.

```typescript
let count: number = 10; let price: number = 9.99;
```

- **String**: Represents sequences of characters.

```typescript
let username: string = "JohnDoe";
```

- **Boolean**: Represents a logical entity and can have two values: `true` or `false`.

```typescript
let isLoggedIn: boolean = true;
```

- **Array**: Represents a collection of values of the same type.

```typescript
let scores: number[] = [90, 85, 100];
```

- **Tuple**: Represents an array with fixed size and known data types for each element.

```typescript
```

```typescript
let player: [string, number] = ["Alice", 25];
```

- **Any**: Represents any kind of value, disabling type checking.

```typescript
let arbitraryValue: any = 42; // Can be changed to any type
```

- **Void**: Represents the absence of a value, often used for functions that do not return a value.

```typescript
function logMessage(message: string): void {
console.log(message);
}
```

1.2. Custom Types

In addition to built-in types, TypeScript allows developers to create custom types using type aliases and union types.

- **Type Aliases**: Create a new name for an existing type.

```typescript
type Point = { x: number; y: number }; let point: Point = {
x: 10, y: 20 };
```

- **Union Types**: Allows a variable to hold more than one type.

```typescript
function formatId(id: number | string): string { return String(id);
}
```

2. Interfaces

Interfaces are one of the primary ways to define the structure of an object in TypeScript. They allow for the definition of contracts within your code, making it clearer what shape the data should take.

2.1. Defining Interfaces

An interface can define properties and methods that can be implemented by classes or objects.

```typescript
interface User {
id: number; username: string;

email?: string; // Optional property
}
const user: User = { id: 1,

username: "JaneDoe",

};


console.log(`User: ${user.username}, ID: ${user.id}`);
```

2.2. Extending Interfaces

You can extend interfaces to create new ones that inherit properties of existing interfaces.

```typescript
interface Admin extends User { accessLevel: string;
}
const admin: Admin = { id: 2,
username: "AdminUser", accessLevel: "full",
};
console.log(`Admin: ${admin.username}, Access Level: ${admin.accessLevel}`);
```

3. Enums

Enums in TypeScript allow for a way to define a set of named constants, providing a way to represent related values in a way that makes your code more readable and maintainable.

3.1. Numeric Enums

Numeric enums are the most common type, where each member is assigned a numeric value.

```typescript
enum Direction {
Up = 1,
Down, Left, Right,
}
let direction: Direction = Direction.Up;
```

```
console.log(direction); // Output: 1
```
` ` `

3.2. String Enums

String enums allow for defining string values, which can be useful for better debugging and logging.

` ` `typescript enum LogLevel {

Info = "INFO", Warn = "WARN", Error = "ERROR",

}

let currentLogLevel: LogLevel = LogLevel.Warn;

console.log(`Current Log Level: ${currentLogLevel}`); // Output: Current Log Level: WARN
` ` `

3.3. Heterogeneous Enums

While not common, TypeScript allows enums to mix numeric and string values.

` ` `typescript enum Mixed {

No = 0,

Yes = "YES",

}

console.log(Mixed.Yes); // Output: YES
` ` `

By understanding and utilizing these features effectively, you can write cleaner, more maintainable, and type-safe code. As you continue your journey with TypeScript, these concepts will become essential tools in your development toolkit, enabling you to build robust applications and take full advantage of the language's capabilities.

Advanced TypeScript Features: Generics, Utility Types, and Mapped Types

In this chapter, we will delve into some of the most advanced features of TypeScript: Generics, Utility Types, and Mapped Types. Understanding these concepts will allow you to leverage TypeScript's full potential and create reusable, type-safe components in your applications.

1. Generics

Generics are one of the most powerful features in TypeScript, allowing you to create functions, classes, and interfaces that work with a variety of types while maintaining type safety. The core idea behind generics is to define a placeholder type that can be replaced with a specific type later.

1.1 Defining and Using Generics

Let's start with a simple example of a generic function. Suppose we want to create a function that returns the first element of an array, regardless of the type of the elements in the array.

```typescript
function getFirstElement<T>(arr: T[]): T { return arr[0];
}

const numberArray = [1, 2, 3];
```

```
const firstNumber = getFirstElement(numberArray); //
firstNumber is 1

const stringArray = ['hello', 'world'];

const firstString = getFirstElement(stringArray); //
firstString is 'hello'
```

In this example, `T` is a generic type parameter that allows the function to work with any type. TypeScript infers the type based on the argument passed, which maintains type safety without losing flexibility.

1.2 Generic Interfaces and Classes

Generics can also be used with interfaces and classes. For instance, you can define a generic interface to represent a simple data structure, like a pair:

```typescript
interface Pair<T, U> { first: T;

second: U;

}

const pair: Pair<number, string> = { first: 42,

second: "forty-two",

};
```

Similarly, you can define a generic class:

```typescript
class Box<T> {

private contents: T;
```

```typescript
  constructor(contents: T) { this.contents = contents;
  }
  getContents(): T { return this.contents;
  }
}
const numberBox = new Box(100); const stringBox = new Box('OpenAI');
```

1.3 Constraining Generics

Sometimes, you may want to restrict the types that can be used as type parameters. This is done using constraints:

```typescript
function logLength<T extends { length: number }>(item: T): void { console.log(item.length);
}
logLength([1, 2, 3]); // Logs: 3 logLength("Hello, World!"); // Logs: 13
// logLength(123); // Error: Argument of type 'number' is not assignable to parameter of type '{ length: number; }'.
```

In this example, we restricted the generic type `T` to be any type that has a `length` property. ## 2. Utility Types

TypeScript provides a set of utility types that help manipulate other types in a simple way. These types are built-in types that can greatly assist in constructing and transforming complex types.

2.1 Common Utility Types

Partial: Makes all properties of a type optional.

Required: Makes all properties of a type required.

Readonly: Makes all properties of a type read-only.

Record: Constructs an object type with properties of a specific type. #### Examples:

```typescript
// Partial interface User {
id: number; name: string; email?: string;
}
const user: Partial<User> = { id: 1,
};
// Required
const userComplete: Required<User> = { id: 1,
name: "John",
email: "john@example.com",
};
// Readonly
const readonlyUser: Readonly<User> = { id: 1,
name: "Jane",
};
readonlyUser.name = "Doe"; // Error: Cannot assign to 'name' because it is a readonly property
// Record
```

```typescript
type UserRoles = 'admin' | 'editor' | 'viewer';

const userAccess: Record<string, UserRoles> = { user1: "admin",

user2: "editor",

};
```

2.2 Exclude and Extract

Two other very useful utility types are `Exclude` and `Extract`, which help manage union types.

```typescript
type NumbersAndStrings = string | number;

type OnlyStrings = Exclude<NumbersAndStrings, number>; // Result: string type OnlyNumbers = Extract<NumbersAndStrings, number>; // Result: number
```

3. Mapped Types

Mapped types allow you to create new types by transforming properties of existing types. This feature is particularly useful when you need to apply changes to many properties in an interface or type.

3.1 Creating Mapped Types

Here's how to create a simple mapped type:

```typescript
type User = { id: number;
```

```typescript
  name: string;
};
type ReadonlyUser = {
  readonly [K in keyof User]: User[K]; // Maps over each
key in User and makes it readonly
};
// Result:
// type ReadonlyUser = {
//   readonly id: number;
//   readonly name: string;
// }
```

3.2 Conditional Properties

You can also create more complex mapped types using conditional types and utility types. For instance, you can create a type that maps properties to their optional counterparts:

```typescript
type Optional<T> = {
  [K in keyof T]?: T[K]; // Makes all properties optional
};
type OptionalUser = Optional<User>;
// Result:
// type OptionalUser = {
```

```
//  id?: number;
//  name?: string;
// }
```
` ` `

3.3 Using Mapped Types with Utility Types

Mapped types can be incredibly powerful when combined with utility types. For example, if you want to create a type that holds the types of all properties in another type, you could do the following:

```typescript
type OriginalType = { a: number;
b: string;
};
type PropertyTypes = {
[K in keyof OriginalType]: OriginalType[K];
};
// Result: { a: number; b: string; }
```
` ` `

By mastering these concepts, you can write more reusable code, enforce stricter type safety, and create data structures that are easier to maintain and extend. As you continue your journey with TypeScript, keep exploring these advanced features, as they can revolutionize the way you design and implement code in your projects.

Chapter 3: Building a Strong Foundation with Node.js and TypeScript

This chapter explores how to effectively leverage Node.js and TypeScript to create a strong architecture that not only meets today's demands but is also adaptable for the future.

3.1 Understanding Node.js

Node.js is a runtime environment that allows developers to execute JavaScript code on the server side. Built on the V8 JavaScript engine developed by Google, Node.js enables developers to build scalable network applications thanks to its non-blocking, event-driven architecture. This architecture makes it particularly well-suited for applications that require real-time capabilities, such as chat applications, streaming services, and collaborative tools.

3.1.1 Key Features of Node.js

Asynchronous and Event-Driven: Node.js uses a non-blocking approach, allowing it to handle multiple connections simultaneously without being bogged down by blocking operations.

Single Programming Language: With Node.js, developers can use JavaScript for both client-side and server-side development, which simplifies the development process and enhances code reusability.

NPM (Node Package Manager): NPM is one of the largest ecosystems of open-source libraries, providing thousands of packages that can speed up development.

3.2 Introducing TypeScript

TypeScript is a superset of JavaScript that adds static typing, interfaces, and other advanced features to the language. Developed by Microsoft, TypeScript is designed to help developers manage large codebases more effectively. Its type system provides additional safety and can catch errors at compile time, reducing potential runtime issues.

3.2.1 Advantages of Using TypeScript

Static Typing: TypeScript allows developers to specify variable types, making the code easier to understand and less prone to errors.

Improved IDE Support: Many IDEs and code editors offer enhanced features when working with TypeScript, including autocompletion, navigation, and documentation, which can significantly improve developer productivity.

Easier Refactoring: TypeScript's type system makes it simpler to refactor code since the compiler can catch type-related issues, allowing developers to make changes with greater confidence.

3.3 Setting Up Your Environment

Before diving into application development, it's essential to set up your environment properly. Here's how to get started with Node.js and TypeScript:

3.3.1 Installing Node.js

To install Node.js, visit the official [Node.js website](https://nodejs.org/) and download the appropriate version for your operating system. Follow the installation instructions, and once installed, verify it by running the following command in your terminal:

```bash
node -v
```

This command should return the version of Node.js you just installed. ### 3.3.2 Setting Up TypeScript

With Node.js installed, you can easily install TypeScript globally using NPM:

```bash
npm install -g typescript
```

To verify that TypeScript is installed, run:

```bash
tsc -v
```

This command will return the installed version of TypeScript. ### 3.3.3 Creating a New Project

Now that your environment is set up, it's time to create a new project. Start by creating a new directory for your project and navigate into it:

```bash
mkdir MyNodeTypeScriptApp cd MyNodeTypeScriptApp
```

Next, initialize a new Node.js project:

```bash npm init -y
```

This command will create a `package.json` file with default configurations. Now install the TypeScript types and the necessary packages for your setup:

```bash
npm install --save-dev typescript @types/node
```

3.3.4 Configuring TypeScript

To configure TypeScript, create a `tsconfig.json` file in your project's root directory. This file enables you to customize various TypeScript compiler options. Here's a basic configuration to get started:

```json
{
"compilerOptions": { "target": "ES6", "module": "commonjs", "strict": true, "esModuleInterop": true, "skipLibCheck": true,

"forceConsistentCasingInFileNames": true
},
"include": ["src/**/*"], "exclude": ["node_modules"]
}
```

This configuration specifies various options, such as the target ECMAScript version, module system, and strict type-checking rules.

45

3.4 Developing Your First Application

Now that you have your environment set up, let's go through the process of developing a simple Node.js application using TypeScript. We'll create a basic HTTP server that responds with a greeting.

3.4.1 Creating the Project Structure

Create a `src` folder within your project directory. This will be the location for your TypeScript source files:

```bash
mkdir src
```

Inside the `src` directory, create a file named `server.ts`:

```bash
touch src/server.ts
```

3.4.2 Writing the Server Code

Open `server.ts` in your favorite code editor and add the following code:

```typescript
import * as http from 'http';

const hostname: string = '127.0.0.1'; const port: number = 3000;

const server = http.createServer((req, res) => {
res.statusCode = 200;

res.setHeader('Content-Type', 'text/plain'); res.end('Hello, World!\n');
});
```

```
server.listen(port, hostname, () => {
  console.log(`Server        running          at
  http://${hostname}:${port}/`);
});
```
```

Here, we import the HTTP module, define the hostname and port, and create a server that responds with "Hello, World!" when accessed.

### 3.4.3 Compiling and Running the Application

To compile the TypeScript code into JavaScript, run the following command:

```bash tsc
```

This command generates a `server.js` file in the same directory as `server.ts`. Now you can run the server using Node.js:

```bash
node src/server.js
```

Visit `http://127.0.0.1:3000` in your browser, and you should see the message "Hello, World!" displayed.

In this chapter, we explored how to build a solid foundation for server-side applications using Node.js and TypeScript. Node.js offers an efficient and scalable runtime for JavaScript, while TypeScript introduces powerful features that enhance code quality and maintainability.
```

Setting Up a TypeScript-Based Node.js Project

Adding TypeScript to the mix can enhance the development experience by providing static typing, interfaces, and modern JavaScript features. This chapter will guide you through the process of setting up a TypeScript-based Node.js project from scratch.

1. Prerequisites

Before we dive into the setup process, ensure that you have the following installed on your machine:

Node.js: Version 12.x or higher (recommended). You can download it from nodejs.org.

npm: This comes installed with Node.js. You can verify the installation by running `npm -v` in your terminal.

TypeScript: We'll install TypeScript along with our project setup. ## 2. Creating a New Node.js Project

Start by creating a new directory for your project:

```bash
mkdir my-typescript-node-app cd my-typescript-node-app
```

Initialize a new Node.js project with npm:

```bash npm init -y
```

This command generates a `package.json` file with default settings. You can modify the fields as needed, but for now, we'll stick with the defaults.

3. Installing TypeScript

Now, let's install TypeScript as a development dependency:

```bash
npm install typescript --save-dev
```

This command installs TypeScript and adds it to your `devDependencies` in `package.json`. To ensure that we have TypeScript ready for configuration, we can check its version:

```bash npx tsc -v
```

4. Initializing TypeScript Configuration

]TypeScript provides a powerful configuration file called `tsconfig.json`. This file is where you specify the compiler options for your project. To create this file automatically, run:

```bash
npx tsc --init
```

This command produces a `tsconfig.json` file in your project directory. Here's a sample configuration that you

49

might find useful:

```json
{
"compilerOptions": {

"target": "ES2020",          // Specify ECMAScript target version "module": "commonjs",                // Specify module code generation "strict": true,    // Enable all strict type-checking options

"esModuleInterop": true,          // Enables emit interoperability between CommonJS and ES Modules "skipLibCheck": true,    // Skip type checking of declaration files "forceConsistentCasingInFileNames": true // Disallow inconsistently-cased references to the same file.

},

"include": ["src/**/*"],    // Specify an array of filenames or patterns to be included in the program "exclude": ["node_modules", "**/*.spec.ts"] // Specify an array of filenames or patterns to be excluded

}
```

Explanation of Key Options

target: We set the ECMAScript version to compile to ES2020 to utilize the latest language features.

module: We use `commonjs` as it's the standard for Node.js.

strict: Activating strict mode increases type safety,

50

which is highly recommended.

esModuleInterop: This option helps when importing modules, making it easier to work with older CommonJS modules.

include: This tells TypeScript where to look for TypeScript files.

exclude: It assists in excluding unnecessary files/folders from the compilation process. ## 5. Setting Up the Project Structure

It's a good practice to organize your project files in a logical structure. Create a `src` folder for all your TypeScript source files:

```bash
mkdir src
```

Inside the `src` directory, create an `index.ts` file, which will serve as the entry point for your application:

```bash
touch src/index.ts
```

You can add a simple hello world code snippet to your `index.ts` file:

```typescript
const express = require('express'); // using CommonJS syntax for now

const app = express(); const port = 3000;

app.get('/', (req, res) => {
```

```
res.send('Hello TypeScript with Node.js!');
});
app.listen(port, () => {
console.log(`Server          is          running          at
http://localhost:${port}`);
});
```
```

## 6. Installing Required Packages

Since we are using Express in our example, we need to install Express and its type definitions:

```bash
npm install express

npm install @types/express --save-dev
```

The first command installs the Express package, while the second one installs the types for Express, allowing TypeScript to recognize types used in the Express library.

If you are using other libraries, remember to install their respective type definitions. ## 7. Adding Build and Start Scripts

Let's add some scripts to our `package.json` to easily build and run our TypeScript application. Edit the `scripts` section of your `package.json` to look like this:

```json "scripts": { "build": "tsc",
"start": "node dist/index.js", "dev": "tsc && node dist/index.js"
```
```

}
```

**build**: This script compiles the TypeScript files into JavaScript.

**start**: This script runs the compiled JavaScript file.

**dev**: This combines both building and starting the app. ## 8. Compiling and Running the Application

Now that everything is set up, you can compile your TypeScript application and start the server. First, run the build command:

```bash

npm run build
```

After building, you can start the application with the following command:


```bash npm start
```

Visit `http://localhost:3000` in your browser, and you should see "Hello TypeScript with Node.js!"

Setting up your TypeScript-based Node.js project! You now have a strong foundation to build more complex applications. As your application grows, consider exploring more TypeScript features like generics, decorators, and modules.
```

Module Systems, ES Modules, and CommonJS in TypeScript

TypeScript, as a superset of JavaScript, not only adopts these module systems but also enriches them with static typing and various other advanced features. This chapter delves into the essential module systems used in TypeScript, focusing on ES Modules (ECMAScript Modules) and CommonJS, their structures, syntax, and practical applications in TypeScript projects.

What are Modules?

At its core, a module is a reusable piece of code contained within its own file. Modules allow developers to separate concerns, improve readability, and manage complexity in larger applications. Both ES Modules and CommonJS serve this purpose in JavaScript, albeit in different contexts and with distinct conventions.

ES Modules (ESM)

Introduced in ECMAScript 2015 (ES6), ES Modules are the standard module system for JavaScript. The ES Module syntax allows developers to export functions, objects, or primitives from a module and import them into other modules. This feature is fundamentally designed for use in web browsers and is also fully supported in Node.js environments.

Syntax

The ES Module syntax uses two primary keywords: `export` and `import`. #### Exporting

You can export variables, functions, or classes from a module in several ways:

Named Exports:

```typescript
// math.ts
export const PI = 3.14;

export function add(a: number, b: number): number {
  return a + b;
}
```

Default Export:

```typescript
// calculator.ts
const subtract = (a: number, b: number): number => {
  return a - b;
};
export default subtract;
```

Importing

You can import exported members into another module as follows:

Importing Named Exports:

```typescript
// main.ts
import { PI, add } from './math'; console.log(PI); // Outputs: 3.14 console.log(add(5, 2)); // Outputs: 7
```

Importing Default Exports:

```typescript
// main.ts
import subtract from './calculator'; console.log(subtract(10, 3)); // Outputs: 7
```

Benefits of ES Modules

Static Structure: Imports and exports are hoisted, leading to more predictable code.

Tree Shaking: Many bundlers can perform tree shaking, removing unused exports from the final build, thus optimizing performance.

Asynchronous Loading: ES Modules can be loaded asynchronously in the browser, improving initial load times.

CommonJS

CommonJS is the module system that has dominated the Node.js ecosystem prior to the adoption of ES Modules. It uses a synchronous module loading mechanism, which makes it suitable for server-side applications where modules are usually loaded from the local filesystem.

Syntax

CommonJS uses two main functions: `require` for importing modules and `module.exports` for exporting them.

Exporting

In CommonJS, you can export a single entity or multiple entities:

Exporting a Single Item:

```javascript
// calculator.js
const subtract = (a, b) => { return a - b;
};
module.exports = subtract;
```

Exporting Multiple Items:

```javascript
// math.js
const PI = 3.14;
const add = (a, b) => { return a + b;
};

module.exports = { PI, add };
```

Importing

To import the exports, you can use the `require` function:

Importing Single Export:

```javascript
// main.js
const      subtract      =      require('./calculator');
console.log(subtract(10, 3)); // Outputs: 7
```

Importing Multiple Exports:

```javascript
// main.js
const math = require('./math'); console.log(math.PI); //
Outputs: 3.14 console.log(math.add(5, 2)); // Outputs: 7
```

Benefits of CommonJS

Simplicity: The syntax is straightforward and easy to understand.

Node.js Compatibility: Since it was designed for server-side JavaScript, most Node.js libraries and tools use CommonJS, ensuring a rich ecosystem.

Using Module Systems in TypeScript

TypeScript supports both ES Modules and CommonJS, enabling developers to choose the one that fits their needs. The choice largely depends on the environment you are targeting—whether it's a browser or Node.js.

Configuring TypeScript for Module Systems

This is managed through the `tsconfig.json` file. You can specify the module system to be used in your compilation.

For ES Modules:

```json
{
"compilerOptions": { "module": "ESNext",

...

}
}
```

For CommonJS:

```json
{
"compilerOptions": { "module": "CommonJS",

...


}
}
```

Interoperability

TypeScript provides interoperability between these module systems. You can import CommonJS modules in an ES Module environment and vice versa using specific TypeScript constructs. This flexibility makes it easier to integrate existing libraries regardless of the module system they are built upon.

Practical Considerations

While developing applications, consider the following:

Choosing a Module System: ES Modules are generally preferred for new projects due to their compatibility with modern development practices, including tree shaking and async loading. CommonJS remains relevant, especially for existing Node.js applications.

Transpilation: Remember that TypeScript transpilation output can differ based on the module system you select. Make sure to test your code, especially when switching between module systems.

Understanding module systems and their implementation in TypeScript is crucial for any developer working in modern JavaScript environments. This chapter highlighted the key differences between ES Modules and CommonJS, their significance, and how to effectively use them in TypeScript projects. Armed with this knowledge, you can ensure that your code is modular, maintainable, and optimized for both performance and usability.

Chapter 4: Working with Express and TypeScript

This chapter will guide you through setting up a TypeScript environment with Express, creating routes, handling middleware, and implementing best practices to ensure your applications are robust and maintainable.

4.1 Setting Up Your Environment

Before we dive into coding, we need to set up our development environment. This involves installing Node.js, initializing a new project, and installing the necessary dependencies.

4.1.1 Installing Node.js

First, ensure that you have Node.js installed on your machine. You can download the latest version from the [official Node.js website](https://nodejs.org/). After installation, verify it by running:

```bash
node -v npm -v
```

4.1.2 Initializing a New Project

Next, create a new directory for your project and initialize it:

```bash
mkdir express-typescript-app cd express-typescript-app npm init -y
```

This command will create a `package.json` file with default values. ### 4.1.3 Installing Express and

61

TypeScript

Now, let's install Express and TypeScript along with the necessary type definitions:

```bash

npm install express

npm install --save-dev typescript @types/node @types/express ts-node nodemon
```

In this command:

`express` is the core framework.

`typescript` adds TypeScript support.

`@types/node` provides type definitions for Node.js.

`@types/express` provides type definitions for Express.

`ts-node` allows us to run TypeScript files directly.

`nodemon` will help in auto-restarting the server during development. ### 4.1.4 Initialize TypeScript Configuration

Now, we need a configuration file for TypeScript. We can create one using the `tsc` command:

```bash

npx tsc --init
```

This will generate a `tsconfig.json` file. Here are some essential settings you might want to include or modify:

```json
```

```
{
"compilerOptions": { "target": "ES6", "module":
"commonjs", "strict": true, "esModuleInterop": true,
"skipLibCheck": true,

"forceConsistentCasingInFileNames": true

},
"include": ["src/**/*.ts"],

"exclude": ["node_modules", "**/*.spec.ts"]

}
```
```

## 4.2 Creating Your First Express App

With the environment set up, let's create a simple Express application. ### 4.2.1 Directory Structure

Create a folder named `src`, which will hold our TypeScript files:

```bash mkdir src
```

4.2.2 Writing Your Express App

Now create a file called `app.ts` inside the `src` directory:

```typescript
// src/app.ts

import express, { Request, Response } from 'express'; const app = express();

const PORT = process.env.PORT || 3000; app.use(express.json()); // Middleware to parse JSON
```
```

bodies

```
app.get('/', (req: Request, res: Response) => {
res.send('Hello, TypeScript with Express!');
});
app.listen(PORT, () => {
console.log(`Server is running on
http://localhost:${PORT}`);
});
```

4.2.3 Running the Application

To run the application, we will use `nodemon` for auto-reloading during development. Update the

`package.json` to add a start script:

```json
"scripts": {
"start": "nodemon -r ts-node/register src/app.ts"
}
```

Now, you can start your application by running:

```bash
npm start
```

Navigate to http://localhost:3000 in your browser. You should see "Hello, TypeScript with Express!". ## 4.3 Exploring Routes and Middleware

Express allows you to handle various HTTP methods and define routes easily. Let's add some more routes and middleware functionalities.

4.3.1 Adding More Routes

In `app.ts`, you can add more routes:

```typescript
app.get('/api/greet', (req: Request, res: Response) => {
res.json({ message: 'Welcome to the Express and TypeScript app!' });
});

app.post('/api/data', (req: Request, res: Response) => {
const { name } = req.body;
res.json({ message: `Hello, ${name}!` });
});
```

4.3.2 Custom Middleware

You can also define custom middleware. For example, logging requests:

```typescript
const logger = (req: Request, res: Response, next: () => void) => { console.log(`${req.method} ${req.url}`);
next();
};
app.use(logger);
```

Add this middleware above your route definitions to log requests. ## 4.4 Error Handling

Error handling is crucial in any application. Express makes it simple to manage errors using middleware. ### 4.4.1 Implementing Error Handling Middleware

You can define a centralized error-handling middleware:

```typescript
app.use((err: any, req: Request, res: Response, next: () =>
void) => { console.error(err.stack);

res.status(500).send('Something went wrong!');

});
```

This middleware should be added at the end of your route definitions to catch errors thrown by other parts of the application.

4.5 Best Practices

4.5.1 Folder Structure

For larger applications, consider organizing your code into separate folders. A common structure might look like this:

```
/src
/controllers
/middlewares
/routes
/models app.ts
```

4.5.2 Typings

Always strive to use TypeScript's strong typing features to define interfaces for your request bodies and responses, making your application robust and self-documenting.

4.5.3 Testing

Implement unit and integration tests to ensure your application behaves as expected. Libraries like Jest and Supertest can be invaluable for this purpose.

By leveraging TypeScript's powerful typing system along with Express's flexible architecture, you can build robust server-side applications that are both maintainable and high-performing.

Creating an Express Server with TypeScript

In the world of web development, building a robust server is a foundational skill. Among the many web frameworks available, Express.js stands out due to its simplicity and powerful features. When combined with TypeScript, a statically typed superset of JavaScript, it enhances the development experience by providing type safety, improved tooling, and better readability.

This chapter will guide you through setting up an Express server using TypeScript step-by-step. By the end of this chapter, you will have a solid understanding of how to create a basic server and some of its essential functionalities.

Prerequisites

Before we dive into the code, ensure that you have the following prerequisites installed on your machine:

Node.js: Download and install Node.js from the official website (https://nodejs.org). This will also install npm (Node Package Manager).

TypeScript: You can install TypeScript globally by running the command:

```bash
npm install -g typescript
```

A Code Editor: Although any text editor can be used, Visual Studio Code (VS Code) is recommended due to its excellent TypeScript support.

Step 1: Setting Up Your Project

Create a new directory for your project and initialize a new Node.js application. Open your terminal and run the following commands:

```bash
mkdir express-typescript-server cd express-typescript-server npm init -y
```

This will create a new directory and generate a `package.json` file with default settings. ## Step 2: Installing Required Packages

Next, we need to install Express and its types, as well as TypeScript and some development tools. Run the following commands:

```bash
npm install express
```

68

```
npm    install   --save-dev   typescript   @types/node
@types/express ts-node nodemon
```
```

Here's a quick description of each package:

**express**: The main framework for building the server.

**@types/node** and **@types/express**: Type definitions for Node.js and Express that allow us to use TypeScript features smoothly.

**typescript**: The TypeScript compiler.

**ts-node**: For running TypeScript files directly.

**nodemon**: A utility that monitors for any changes in your source files and automatically restarts your server.

## Step 3: Configuring TypeScript

In the project root directory, create a new file named `tsconfig.json`. This file will contain the configuration for TypeScript. Add the following content to it:

```json
{

"compilerOptions": { "target": "ES6", "module": "commonjs", "strict": true, "esModuleInterop": true, "skipLibCheck": true,

"forceConsistentCasingInFileNames": true, "outDir": "./dist"

},

"include": ["src/**/*"], "exclude": ["node_modules"]

}
```
```

```
` ` `
```

Explanation of `tsconfig.json` options:

target: Specifies the output language level (ES6 in our case).

module: Specifies the module system to use (CommonJS for Node.js).

strict: Enables all strict type-checking options.

esModuleInterop: Allows for mixing CommonJS and ES Modules.

skipLibCheck: Skips type checking of declaration files.

outDir: Specifies the output directory for compiled files.

include and **exclude**: Specifies which files to include in the compilation process. ## Step 4: Creating the Server

Now, create a new directory called `src` where we will keep our source files. Inside the `src` directory, create a file named `server.ts`. This file will house our Express server code.

Sample Code for `server.ts`

```typescript
import express, { Request, Response } from 'express';

const app = express();

const PORT = process.env.PORT || 3000;

// Middleware to parse JSON bodies
app.use(express.json());
```

```
// A simple route
app.get('/', (req: Request, res: Response) => {
res.send('Welcome to the Express server built with
TypeScript!');
});
// Start the server app.listen(PORT, () => {
console.log(`Server          is          running          on
http://localhost:${PORT}`);
});
```

Explanation of the Code:

import statements: Importing necessary modules and types.

app: Initializing an instance of Express.

Middleware: Using `express.json()` to handle JSON requests.

Route: Defining a simple GET route that responds with a message.

app.listen(): Starting the server and listening on the specified port. ## Step 5: Running the Server

To run your server, you can add a script in your `package.json`:

```json
"scripts": {
"start": "nodemon src/server.ts"
```

```
}
```
```
```

Now, in the terminal, run the following command:

```bash npm start
```
```
```

You should see an output indicating that your server is running. Open your browser and navigate to

`http://localhost:3000` to see the welcome message. ## Step 6: Adding Some Features

A Post Route

To demonstrate how to handle different HTTP methods, let's add a POST route that accepts JSON data. Update your `server.ts` as follows:

```typescript
app.post('/api/data', (req: Request, res: Response) => {
const { name, age } = req.body;

// Normally you'd process the data, save to database, etc.
res.json({ message: `Received data for ${name}, Age: ${age}` });

});
```
```
```

This route will listen for POST requests on `/api/data` and respond with a message containing the received data.

Testing the Post Route

You can use tools like Postman or cURL to test this new route. For example, using cURL in your terminal, you could run:

```bash
curl -X POST http://localhost:3000/api/data -H "Content-Type: application/json" -d '{"name":"John", "age":30}'
```

You should receive a JSON response echoing back the received data.

In this chapter, we walked through the process of creating a basic Express server using TypeScript. We set up the project, configured TypeScript, added routes, and tested our server. With this foundational knowledge, you can now start exploring more advanced features of Express and TypeScript.

Middleware, Routing, and Request Handling in TypeScript

This chapter will explore these concepts in-depth, particularly focusing on how they can be implemented using TypeScript. By leveraging TypeScript's capabilities, we can build more robust, type-safe, and maintainable applications.

1. What is Middleware?

Middleware refers to functions that have access to the request object (req), the response object (res), and the next middleware function in the application's request-response cycle. This provides a powerful way to extend application functionality across multiple routes.

1.1 Characteristics of Middleware

Composability: Middleware functions can be composed together, allowing developers to define stack-like behaviors.

Reusability: Once created, middleware can be reused across multiple routes or even different applications.

Asynchronous Support: Middleware can support both synchronous and asynchronous processes, making it versatile for handling various tasks.

1.2 Types of Middleware

Application-Level Middleware: These are bound to an instance of an Express application (`app.use`).

Router-Level Middleware: These are bound to an instance of a router.

Error Handling Middleware: These handle errors thrown in the application, allowing for centralized error management.

Built-in Middleware: Middleware provided by frameworks such as Express, for instance,

`express.json()` for parsing JSON request bodies. ### Example of Middleware in TypeScript

```typescript
import express, { Request, Response, NextFunction } from 'express'; const app = express();

// Logger middleware

app.use((req: Request, res: Response, next: NextFunction)
```

```
=> { console.log(`${req.method} ${req.url}`);
next(); // Pass control to the next middleware
});
// JSON parser middleware app.use(express.json());
```
```

## 2. Understanding Routing

Routing refers to the processes that determine how an application responds to client requests to specific endpoints, defined by a URI (or path) and a specific HTTP method (GET, POST, DELETE, etc.).

### 2.1 Router in Express.js

Express provides a router object that allows you to create modular, mountable route handlers. A typical usage of the router would involve defining routes to handle various HTTP methods.

```typescript
import { Router } from 'express'; const router = Router();

router.get('/users', (req: Request, res: Response) => {
res.send('List of users');
});

router.post('/users', (req: Request, res: Response) => {
const newUser = req.body;

// Logic to create a user

res.status(201).send(`User created: ${newUser.name}`);
});

export default router;
```
```

```
```

2.2 Parameterized Routes

TypeScript and Express allow you to define dynamic routes that can capture URL parameters.

```typescript
router.get('/users/:id', (req: Request, res: Response) => {
const userId = req.params.id;

res.send(`Details for user ${userId}`);

});
```

3. Request Handling

Once the routing directs a request to a specific handler, that handler must manage the request appropriately—validating inputs, processing data, interacting with databases, and forming responses.

3.1 Request Object

The `Request` object contains vital information about the incoming request, including headers, body, and query parameters. Using TypeScript, we can create interfaces to enforce strong typing on the request body.

```typescript interface User {

name: string; email: string;

}

router.post('/users', (req: Request<{}, {}, User>, res: Response) => { const user: User = req.body;

// Process user creation...
```

```typescript
res.status(201).json({ message: 'User created successfully',
user });
```

```
});
```
` ` `

3.2 Handling Responses

Responses are typically sent back to the client using the `Response` object. This includes setting status codes, headers, and body content.

` ` `typescript

```typescript
router.get('/users', (req: Request, res: Response) => {
```

```typescript
const users = []; // Imagine this array comes from a
database res.status(200).json(users);
```

```
});
```
` ` `

3.3 Error Handling

A crucial part of request handling is managing errors gracefully. Express allows you to define error-handling middleware that can catch and process errors occurring in your routes.

` ` `typescript

```typescript
app.use((err: Error, req: Request, res: Response, next:
NextFunction) => { console.error(err.stack);
```

```typescript
res.status(500).json({ message: 'Internal Server Error!' });
```

```
});
```
` ` `

By utilizing middleware, developers can create a chain of functions that serve to preprocess requests, route them appropriately, and handle responses and errors systematically. The type safety provided by TypeScript enhances these processes, making them more reliable and easier to maintain. In the following chapters, we will explore more advanced features and best practices that leverage these concepts to build scalable applications.

Chapter 5: API Development with TypeScript and Express

This chapter will delve into the essentials of building APIs using TypeScript with the Express framework, focusing on creating a maintainable and scalable architecture.

5.1 Introduction to TypeScript and Express ### 5.1.1 What is TypeScript?

TypeScript is a statically typed superset of JavaScript that compiles down to plain JavaScript. It offers features such as strong typing, interfaces, and advanced tooling, which can significantly enhance the development experience and maintainability of your code.

5.1.2 What is Express?

Express is a minimal and flexible Node.js web application framework that provides a robust set of features for web and mobile applications. It simplifies routing, middleware integration, and handling of requests and responses.

5.1.3 Why Use TypeScript with Express?

The combination of TypeScript and Express brings together strong typing and a robust web framework, providing benefits such as:

Improved developer experience through type safety.

Enhanced code quality and maintainability.

Easier debugging and refactoring due to static typing.

A rich ecosystem of libraries and middleware compatible with Express. ## 5.2 Setting Up Your Development Environment

5.2.1 Installing Node.js and TypeScript

To begin with, ensure you have Node.js installed on your machine. You can download it from [Node.js official website](https://nodejs.org). Once installed, use npm (Node Package Manager) to install TypeScript globally:

```bash
npm install -g typescript
```

5.2.2 Creating a New Project

Start by creating a new directory for your API project:

```bash
mkdir my-api cd my-api
```

Next, initialize a new Node.js project:

```bash npm init -y
```

5.2.3 Installing Express and TypeScript Types Install Express and its type definitions:

```bash
npm install express

npm install --save-dev @types/express
```

You may also want to install additional types for Node.js:

```bash

80
```

```
npm install --save-dev @types/node
```

5.2.4 Setting Up TypeScript Configuration

Create a `tsconfig.json` file in the root directory of your project to set TypeScript compilation options:

```json
{
"compilerOptions": { "target": "ES6", "module": "commonjs", "outDir": "./dist",
"rootDir": "./src", "strict": true, "esModuleInterop": true
},
"include": ["src/**/*"], "exclude": ["node_modules"]
}
```

5.3 Creating Your First API ### 5.3.1 Project Structure

Create the following directory structure within your project:

```
my-api/ src/
index.ts tsconfig.json package.json
```

5.3.2 Writing the API Code

In `src/index.ts`, set up a basic Express server:

81

```typescript
import express from 'express';

const app = express(); const PORT = 3000;

// Middleware for parsing JSON requests
app.use(express.json());

// Sample endpoint app.get('/api', (req, res) => {

res.json({ message: 'Hello, World!' });

});

// Start the server app.listen(PORT, () => {

console.log(`Server is running on
http://localhost:${PORT}`);

});
```

5.3.3 Running the API

Add scripts to your `package.json` to compile and run the application:

```json
"scripts": {

"build": "tsc",

"start": "node dist/index.js", "dev": "ts-node src/index.ts"

}
```

For development purposes, you can use `ts-node`, allowing you to run TypeScript files directly:

```bash
```

```
npm install --save-dev ts-node
```

Now you can start your server:

```bash
npm run dev
```

Visit `http://localhost:3000/api` in your browser, and you should see a JSON response: `{"message": "Hello, World!"}`.

5.4 Developing RESTful Endpoints ### 5.4.1 CRUD Operations

In this section, we will expand our API to support basic CRUD (Create, Read, Update, Delete) operations. For this, let's assume we are managing a list of users.

5.4.2 User Model

First, create a `User` interface in a new file `src/models/User.ts`:

```typescript
export interface User { id: number;

name: string; email: string;

}
```

5.4.3 In-Memory Data Store

Next, create an in-memory array to hold user data in `src/index.ts`:

```typescript
let users: User[] = [];
```

5.4.4 Implementing the Endpoints Add endpoints for CRUD operations:

```typescript
// Create a new user app.post('/api/users', (req, res) => {
const user: User = req.body;
user.id = users.length + 1; // Simple ID generation users.push(user);
res.status(201).json(user);
});
// Get all users app.get('/api/users', (req, res) => {
res.json(users);
});
// Get a user by ID app.get('/api/users/:id', (req, res) => {
const id = parseInt(req.params.id);
const user = users.find(u => u.id === id); if (user) {
res.json(user);
} else {
res.status(404).send('User not found');
}
});
// Update a user app.put('/api/users/:id', (req, res) => {
```

```
const id = parseInt(req.params.id);
const index = users.findIndex(u => u.id === id); if (index
!== -1) {


users[index]    =    {    ...users[index],    ...req.body    };
res.json(users[index]);
} else {
res.status(404).send('User not found');
}
});
// Delete a user app.delete('/api/users/:id', (req, res) => {
const id = parseInt(req.params.id); users = users.filter(u
=> u.id !== id); res.status(204).send(); // No content
});
```

5.4.5 Testing Your API

You can use tools like Postman or cURL to test your API
endpoints. For example, to create a user, make a POST
request to `http://localhost:3000/api/users` with a
JSON body like:

```json
{
"name": "John Doe",
"email": "john@example.com"
}
```

```
```

5.5 Error Handling and Middlewares ### 5.5.1 Error Handling Middleware

It's essential to handle errors gracefully. You can create a simple error-handling middleware:

```typescript

app.use((err, req, res, next) => { console.error(err.stack);
res.status(500).send('Something broke!');

});
```

5.5.2 Validation Middleware

You should also validate requests. A library like `express-validator` can help:

```bash

npm install express-validator
```

You can then use it in your routes to validate incoming data. ## 5.6 Testing Your API

5.6.1 Unit Testing

Using a testing framework like Jest or Mocha will allow you to write unit tests for your API. Start by installing Jest:

```bash

npm install --save-dev jest ts-jest @types/jest
```

Create a `tests` directory and write tests for your endpoints. For example:

```typescript
// tests/user.test.ts
import request from 'supertest';
import app from '../src/index'; // Ensure this exports the Express app
describe('User API', () => {
it('should create a new user', async () => { const res = await request(app)
.post('/api/users')
.send({ name: 'Jane Doe', email: 'jane@example.com' });

expect(res.status).toBe(201);
expect(res.body.name).toBe('Jane Doe');
});
});
```

To run your tests, add a testing script in `package.json`:

```json
"test": "jest"
```

Then execute:

```bash
npm test
```

5.7 Conclusion

We set up a basic project structure, implemented CRUD operations for a user resource, and discussed adding error handling and validation. With TypeScript's strong typing and Express's flexibility, developing APIs can be a seamless experience.

Designing and Structuring a RESTful API

With the rise of microservices and the need for scalable and maintainable applications, understanding how to design a RESTful API that adheres to principles of representational state transfer (REST) is crucial.

TypeScript, a superset of JavaScript, adds static typing to the mix, enabling developers to write more maintainable and error-free code. This chapter will guide you through the process of designing and structuring a RESTful API using TypeScript.

What is a RESTful API?

Before we dive into the practical aspects, it's essential to understand what RESTful APIs are. REST (Representational State Transfer) is an architectural style that allows communication between clients and servers over HTTP. A RESTful API exposes a set of endpoints (URLs) that correspond to resources, enabling clients to perform CRUD (Create, Read, Update, Delete) operations.

Principles of REST

To design an efficient RESTful API, it's vital to adhere to the following principles:

Statelessness: Each request from the client to the server must contain all the necessary information to fulfill the request.

Resource-Based: APIs should expose resources (data models), which clients can interact with via standard HTTP methods (GET, POST, PUT, DELETE).

Representation: Resources can have multiple representations (e.g., JSON, XML), but JSON is commonly favored due to its simplicity and compatibility with JavaScript.

Hypermedia as the Engine of Application State (HATEOAS): Clients should be able to navigate the API's resources dynamically through hyperlinks provided in responses.

Setting Up the TypeScript Environment

Before we start coding our RESTful API, let's set up the environment.

Install Node.js: Ensure you have Node.js installed on your machine. You can download it from nodejs.org.

Initialize a TypeScript project:

```bash
mkdir my-rest-api cd my-rest-api npm init -y

npm install typescript ts-node express @types/node @types/express npx tsc --init
```

Create Directory Structure:

```bash
mkdir src
touch src/index.ts
```

Building the RESTful API

Now, let's create a simple RESTful API for managing a list of books. This example will involve implementing all CRUD operations.

Step 1: Setting Up the Server

In `src/index.ts`, we will set up a basic Express server:

```typescript
import express, { Request, Response } from 'express';
const app = express();
const PORT = process.env.PORT || 3000;
// Middleware app.use(express.json());
// Start the server app.listen(PORT, () => {
console.log(`Server is running on http://localhost:${PORT}`);
});
```

Step 2: Defining Book Model

Create a new file `src/models/Book.ts` to define the data structure:

```typescript
export interface Book { id: number;
title: string; author: string;
publishedYear: number;
}
```

Step 3: In-Memory Database

For simplicity, we will use an in-memory array to simulate a database. Create `src/data/books.ts`:

```typescript
import { Book } from '../models/Book';

let books: Book[] = []; let currentId = 1;

export const getBooks = () => books;

export const getBookById = (id: number) =>
books.find(book => book.id === id); export const
addBook = (book: Omit<Book, 'id'>) => {

const newBook = { id: currentId++, ...book };
books.push(newBook);

return newBook;
};

export const updateBook = (id: number, updatedBook:
Partial<Book>) => { const index = books.findIndex(book
=> book.id === id);

if (index === -1) return null;
```

91

```typescript
  books[index] = { ...books[index], ...updatedBook }; return
  books[index];
};
export const deleteBook = (id: number) => {
  const index = books.findIndex(book => book.id === id); if
  (index !== -1) {
    books.splice(index, 1); return true;
  }
  return false;
};
```

Step 4: Implementing API Endpoints

Now, let's implement the CRUD endpoints in `src/index.ts`:

```typescript
import { addBook, deleteBook, getBookById, getBooks,
updateBook } from './data/books';
// Get all books
app.get('/api/books', (req: Request, res: Response) => {
  res.json(getBooks());
});
// Get book by ID
app.get('/api/books/:id', (req: Request, res: Response) =>
{ const book = getBookById(parseInt(req.params.id));
  if (book) { res.json(book);
```

```
  } else {

  res.status(404).json({ message: 'Book not found' });

  }

});

// Add a new book

app.post('/api/books', (req: Request, res: Response) => {
const      newBook      =      addBook(req.body);
res.status(201).json(newBook);

});

// Update a book

app.put('/api/books/:id', (req: Request, res: Response) =>
{

const                  updatedBook                  =
updateBook(parseInt(req.params.id),    req.body);    if
(updatedBook) {

res.json(updatedBook);

} else {

res.status(404).json({ message: 'Book not found' });

}

});

// Delete a book

app.delete('/api/books/:id', (req: Request, res: Response)
=> { const deleted = deleteBook(parseInt(req.params.id));

if (deleted) { res.status(204).send();

} else {
```

```
res.status(404).json({ message: 'Book not found' });
}
});
```

Testing the API

To test the API, you may use tools like Postman, Insomnia, or curl commands to send requests to your API endpoints:

GET `/api/books` - Retrieve all books

GET `/api/books/{id}` - Retrieve a book by ID

POST `/api/books` - Add a new book (send a JSON body with title, author, publishedYear)

PUT `/api/books/{id}` - Update an existing book

DELETE `/api/books/{id}` - Delete a book ### Error Handling and Validation

In a production environment, you'll also want to include error handling and validation. For example, using a library like `Joi` or `express-validator`, you can validate incoming data to ensure it meets the required schema.

We explored the foundational aspects of designing and structuring a RESTful API using TypeScript. By following REST principles and leveraging the capabilities of TypeScript, we can create APIs that are not only functional but also maintainable and scalable.

Validating and Handling Requests with TypeScript

TypeScript enhances the process by adding strong typing to JavaScript, leading to fewer runtime errors and clearer code intentions. This chapter delves into validating and handling requests effectively using TypeScript, particularly in the context of building RESTful APIs.

1. Understanding the Need for Validation

Before we dive into the implementation, it's crucial to understand why validation is necessary. When your application exposes an API, it acts as a gateway for external interactions. Requests may come from various sources, including third-party services, user interfaces, or microservices. Each request can contain data that, if not carefully validated, could lead to security vulnerabilities like SQL injection, denial-of-service attacks, or corrupt data being stored in your database.

1.1 Types of Validation

Validation can be categorized into several types:

Type Checking: Ensuring the type of data matches the expected types.

Structural Validation: Checking that the data matches a defined structure (i.e., required properties are present).

Value Validation: Ensuring that values fit within allowed ranges or formats.

Business Logic Validation: Ensuring that the data adheres to specific business rules. ## 2. Setting Up a

TypeScript Environment

To implement validation in TypeScript, you first need a functional TypeScript project. This typically includes setting up Node.js, TypeScript, and an HTTP framework such as Express.

Initialize a Node.js Project:

```bash

mkdir typescript-request-validation cd typescript-request-validation npm init -y

```

Install TypeScript and Necessary Libraries:

```bash

npm install typescript ts-node express body-parser @types/node @types/express

```

Create a TypeScript Configuration File: Generate a `tsconfig.json` file.

```json
{

"compilerOptions": { "target": "ES6", "module": "commonjs", "strict": true, "esModuleInterop": true, "skipLibCheck": true,


"forceConsistentCasingInFileNames": true
},
"include": ["src/**/*"]
```

```
}
```

Set Up a Basic Express Server:

Create a `src/index.ts` file.

```typescript
import express from 'express';

const app = express(); const PORT = 3000;

app.use(express.json()); app.listen(PORT, () => {

console.log(`Server          is          running          on
http://localhost:${PORT}`);

});
```

3. Validating Requests

With the server set up, we can now focus on validating incoming requests. For this purpose, we can use libraries like `Joi` or `Yup`. Here, we'll use `Joi` for its powerful schema-based validation.

3.1 Installing Joi

```bash
npm install joi @types/joi
```

3.2 Creating Validation Schemas

First, let's define a data structure for a hypothetical user registration.

```typescript
```

```typescript
// src/schemas/userSchema.ts import Joi from 'joi';
export const userSchema = Joi.object({
username: Joi.string().alphanum().min(3).max(30).required(),
password: Joi.string().pattern(new RegExp('^[a-zA-Zo-9]{3,30}$')).required(),                email: Joi.string().email().required(),
});
```

3.3 Implementing Validation Middleware

Next, create middleware to validate incoming requests. This middleware will use the schema we defined earlier.

```typescript
// src/middleware/validateRequest.ts


import { Request, Response, NextFunction } from 'express'; import { userSchema } from '../schemas/userSchema';
export const validateUserRequest = (req: Request, res: Response, next: NextFunction) => { const { error } = userSchema.validate(req.body);


if (error) {
return res.status(400).json({ status: 'fail',
message: error.details[0].message,
});
```

```
}

next();

};

` ` `
```

3.4 Integrating Middleware into Your Express Routes

Now we can use this middleware in our Express application:

```typescript
// src/routes/userRoutes.ts import express from 'express';

import { validateUserRequest } from '../middleware/validateRequest'; const router = express.Router();

router.post('/register', validateUserRequest, (req, res) => {

// Logic to register the user would go here return res.status(201).json({

status: 'success', data: {

// Return user information (excluding sensitive details) username: req.body.username,

email: req.body.email,

},

});

});

export default router;
```

```
```

Finally, include this route in your main server file:

```typescript
// src/index.ts
import express from 'express';
import userRoutes from './routes/userRoutes';
const app = express(); const PORT = 3000;
app.use(express.json()); app.use('/api', userRoutes);
app.listen(PORT, () => {
console.log(`Server is running on http://localhost:${PORT}`);
});
```

4. Handling Errors Gracefully

While validating data is essential, it is equally important to handle errors gracefully. A well-structured error response can help clients understand what went wrong and how to fix it.

4.1 Custom Error Handling Middleware

Create an error handling middleware to handle unexpected errors and provide user-friendly messages.

```typescript
// src/middleware/errorHandler.ts
import { Request, Response, NextFunction } from 'express';
```

```typescript
export const errorHandler = (err: Error, req: Request, res:
Response,      next:      NextFunction)      =>      {
console.error(err.stack);

res.status(500).json({ status: 'error',

message: 'Something went wrong!',

});

};
```

4.2 Using the Error Handling Middleware

To integrate this middleware into your application, append it after your route definitions:

```typescript
// src/index.ts

import      {      errorHandler      }      from
'./middleware/errorHandler';

// ... existing imports

app.use('/api', userRoutes); app.use(errorHandler);
```

In this chapter, we've covered the importance of request validation in web applications and how TypeScript, along with libraries like Joi, can enhance your ability to securely and effectively manage incoming data.

Validating requests not only protects your application from malicious inputs but also ensures that your API remains reliable and easy to use.

Chapter 6: Database Integration in TypeScript Backend

This chapter delves into the intricacies of database integration in a TypeScript backend, focusing on popular database technologies, ORMs, and best practices for managing data efficiently and consistently.

6.1 Understanding Database Options

Before diving into the integration process, it's imperative to understand the various database options available. Broadly, databases can be categorized into two types: **relational** and **non-relational (NoSQL)**.

6.1.1 Relational Databases

Relational databases, such as PostgreSQL and MySQL, store data in structured tables with defined relationships. They follow a schema that ensures data integrity and can leverage SQL for querying.

Pros:

Strong consistency guarantees

Robust querying capabilities

Support for ACID transactions

Cons:

Requires more upfront schema definition

Less flexible in terms of data structure changes ### 6.1.2 Non-Relational Databases

Non-relational databases, such as MongoDB and Redis, offer more flexibility with their schema-less design. They store data in various formats like key-value pairs, documents, or graphs.

Pros:

Highly scalable and flexible

Faster write operations

Cons:

Weaker consistency models

Variability in querying capabilities ### 6.1.3 Choosing the Right Database

The choice between relational and non-relational databases should be driven by the specific needs of the application. Consider aspects such as data structure, the need for transactions, scalability requirements, and team familiarity with the technology.

6.2 Setting Up the TypeScript Backend

After selecting the appropriate database, setting up your TypeScript backend is the next step. Here's how to start with a basic Express server integrated with a PostgreSQL database using the TypeORM library.

6.2.1 Installing Necessary Packages

To begin, ensure you have Node.js and TypeScript installed. Then, create your project directory and install the required packages:

```bash npm init -y
```

npm install express typeorm pg reflect-metadata

npm install @types/express @types/node typescript ts-node --save-dev

```
```

6.2.2 Configuring TypeScript

Create a `tsconfig.json` file with the necessary configurations for your project:

```json
{
"compilerOptions": { "target": "ES6", "module": "commonjs", "strict": true, "esModuleInterop": true, "skipLibCheck": true,
"forceConsistentCasingInFileNames": true, "outDir": "./dist"
},
"include": ["src/**/*"], "exclude": ["node_modules"]
}
```

6.2.3 Establishing the Database Connection

Next, set up the database connection. Create a new folder named `src` and inside it, create a file called

`app.ts`:

```typescript
import "reflect-metadata";

import { createConnection } from "typeorm"; import express from "express";

const app = express(); const PORT = 3000;

createConnection().then(() => { app.listen(PORT, () => {
```

```
console.log(`Server         is         running         on
http://localhost:${PORT}`);
});

}).catch(error => console.log(error));
```

You will need to create a `ormconfig.json` file in the root of your project to define your database connection settings:

```json
{
"type": "postgres",

"host": "localhost", "port": 5432,

"username": "your-username", "password": "your-password", "database": "your-database", "synchronize": true, "logging": false,

"entities": ["src/entity/**/*.ts"]

}
```

6.2.4 Creating Entities

Entities in TypeORM are essentially classes that map to database tables. Create a new folder named `entity` in `src` and define a sample entity, such as `User.ts`:

```typescript
import { Entity, PrimaryGeneratedColumn, Column } from "typeorm";
```

```typescript
@Entity()
export class User { @PrimaryGeneratedColumn() id: number;

@Column() name: string;

@Column() email: string;

}
```

6.2.5 Handling CRUD Operations

To manage CRUD operations effectively, incorporate routes into your application. Here's how to implement basic CRUD for the `User` entity:

```typescript
import { getRepository } from "typeorm"; import { User } from "./entity/User";

// Create a new user
app.post("/users", async (req, res) => {

const userRepository = getRepository(User); const user = userRepository.create(req.body);                    await userRepository.save(user); res.status(201).send(user);

});

// Get all users
app.get("/users", async (req, res) => {

const userRepository = getRepository(User); const users = await userRepository.find(); res.status(200).send(users);

});
```

```
// Update a user
app.put("/users/:id", async (req, res) => { const
userRepository = getRepository(User);

await userRepository.update(req.params.id, req.body);

const          updatedUser          =          await
userRepository.findOne(req.params.id);
res.status(200).send(updatedUser);

});

// Delete a user
app.delete("/users/:id", async (req, res) => { const
userRepository    =    getRepository(User);    await
userRepository.delete(req.params.id);
res.status(204).send();

});
```

6.3 Error Handling and Validation

Error handling and input validation are critical in any application. Use middleware to validate incoming requests and handle errors gracefully.

6.3.1 Using Middleware for Validation

You can use libraries like `express-validator` to validate user input:

```bash
npm install express-validator
```

In your route, you can add validation rules before

processing the request:

```typescript
import { check, validationResult } from "express-validator";

app.post("/users",                                    [
check("name").isString().not().isEmpty(),
check("email").isEmail(),

], async (req, res) => {

const errors = validationResult(req); if (!errors.isEmpty()) {

return res.status(400).json({ errors: errors.array() });

}

// Proceed with user creation...

});
```

6.3.2 Global Error Handling

Set up a global error-handling middleware to capture any unforeseen errors:

```typescript
app.use((err, req, res, next) => { console.error(err.stack);
res.status(500).send('Something went wrong!');

});
```

6.4 Testing Your Application

Testing is a vital part of the development process. With

your TypeScript backend set up, consider using frameworks like Jest for unit testing your API.

```bash
npm install --save-dev jest ts-jest @types/jest
```

Create test cases for your routes, ensuring that CRUD operations perform as expected. Testing your application will help maintain code quality and catch regression issues early.

Database integration in a TypeScript backend is a powerful technique that enables developers to manage data effectively. This chapter covered various database options, set up a basic Express server with PostgreSQL integration using TypeORM, and discussed validation and error handling best practices.

The world of backend development is vast, and mastering these concepts will set the foundation for building robust applications in a scalable and efficient manner.

Using TypeORM, Prisma, and Mongoose with TypeScript

This chapter delves into three of the most popular libraries used for integrating databases into TypeScript backend applications: TypeORM, Prisma, and Mongoose. We will explore their unique features, advantages, and use cases, guiding you through setting them up in your application.

1. Understanding the Tools ### 1.1 TypeORM

TypeORM is an ORM for TypeScript and JavaScript (ES7, ES6, ES5). It supports various databases, including PostgreSQL, MySQL, SQLite, and more. With TypeORM, developers can define models (entities) using TypeScript classes and decorators, simplifying the process of working with databases.

Key Features:

Support for Active Record and Data Mapper patterns.

Built-in support for migrations.

Eager and lazy loading.

Support for relations (One-to-One, One-to-Many, Many-to-One, Many-to-Many).

Extensive query methods and entity listeners. ### 1.2 Prisma

Prisma is a modern ORM that focuses on providing a comfortable developer experience. It generates a type- safe query builder based on your database schema, providing autocompletion and type inference. Prisma supports various databases, including PostgreSQL, MySQL, SQLite, and MongoDB.

Key Features:

Type safety: Provides types inferred from your database schema.

Prisma Migrate: A robust migration system.

Prisma Client: An auto-generated query builder.

Easy integration with existing databases. ### 1.3

Mongoose

Mongoose is an ODM specifically for MongoDB and Node.js. It provides a straightforward way to model

your application data, enforce schema validation, and interact with MongoDB databases.

Key Features:

Schema definitions with validation.

Middleware support for data manipulation.

Population feature for model relationships.

Plugins to extend functionality.

2. Setting Up Your Development Environment

Before diving into examples, you need to set up your development environment. Follow these steps to create a TypeScript project using Node.js.

2.1 Create a New Project

```bash
mkdir ts-backend-example cd ts-backend-example npm init -y
```

2.2 Install TypeScript and Required Packages

Install TypeScript, along with the Type definitions and the libraries you want to use (TypeORM, Prisma, and Mongoose).

```bash
npm install typescript ts-node @types/node --save-dev

npm install typeorm reflect-metadata mysql2 // For
TypeORM with MySQL npm install @prisma/client
prisma // For Prisma

npm install mongoose @types/mongoose // For
Mongoose
```

2.3 Initialize TypeScript Configuration

Create a `tsconfig.json` file with the following settings:

```json
{
"compilerOptions": { "target": "ES6", "module":
"commonjs", "strict": true, "esModuleInterop": true,
"skipLibCheck": true,

"forceConsistentCasingInFileNames": true

},

"include": ["src/**/*"], "exclude": ["node_modules"]

}
```

3. Using TypeORM with TypeScript ### 3.1 Setting Up
TypeORM

Create a `src` folder and an `entity` folder within it.

Create an `ormconfig.json` file for your database
configuration:

```json
{
"type": "mysql",
"host": "localhost",
"username": "root", "password": "password", "database":
"test", "synchronize": true,
"logging": true, "entities": [ "dist/entity/**/*.js"
],
"migrations": [ "dist/migration/**/*.js"
],
"cli": {
"entitiesDir":          "src/entity",          "migrationsDir":
"src/migration"
}
}
```

Define a sample entity (e.g., `User.ts`):

```typescript
import { Entity, PrimaryGeneratedColumn, Column }
from "typeorm";
@Entity()
export class User { @PrimaryGeneratedColumn() id:
number;
@Column() name: string;
```

113

```typescript
@Column() email: string;
}
```

Create a connection and a sample query in `index.ts`:

```typescript
import "reflect-metadata";

import { createConnection } from "typeorm"; import {
User } from "./entity/User";

createConnection().then(async connection => {

const userRepository = connection.getRepository(User);

// Create a new user

const newUser = userRepository.create({ name: "John
Doe", email: "john.doe@example.com" }); await
userRepository.save(newUser);

console.log("New User Saved:", newUser);

}).catch(error => console.log(error));
```

3.2 Running the Application Execute your TypeScript application:

```bash
npx ts-node src/index.ts
```

4. Using Prisma with TypeScript ### 4.1 Setting Up Prisma

Initialize Prisma in your project:

```bash
npx prisma init
```

This command creates a `prisma` folder with a `schema.prisma` file, where you define your data model.

Define your schema in `schema.prisma`:

```prisma
datasource db {
provider = "mysql"
url     = env("DATABASE_URL")
}
generator client {
provider = "prisma-client-js"
}
model User {
id    Int    @id    @default(autoincrement())    name String
email String @unique
}
```

Update your `.env` file with your database connection string:

```
DATABASE_URL="mysql://root:password@localhost:330
6/test"
```

Run the migration:

```bash
npx prisma migrate dev --name init
```

Use the Prisma Client in an `index.ts` file:

```typescript
import { PrismaClient } from '@prisma/client'; const
prisma = new PrismaClient();

async function main() {
const user = await prisma.user.create({ data: {
name: 'Jane Doe',
email: 'jane.doe@example.com'
}
});
console.log('New User Created:', user);
}
main()
.catch(e => console.error(e))
.finally(async () => {
```

```
await prisma.$disconnect();
});
```

4.2 Running the Application Execute the application again:

```bash
npx ts-node src/index.ts
```

5. Using Mongoose with TypeScript ### 5.1 Setting Up Mongoose

Create a model in `models/User.ts`:

```typescript
import mongoose, { Document, Schema } from 'mongoose';

export interface IUser extends Document { name: string;

email: string;

}

const UserSchema: Schema = new Schema({ name: { type: String, required: true }, email: { type: String, required: true }

});

export const User = mongoose.model<IUser>('User', UserSchema);
```

Connect to MongoDB in `index.ts`:

117

```typescript
import mongoose from 'mongoose';
import { User, IUser } from './models/User';

async function main() {
await mongoose.connect('mongodb://localhost:27017/test');
const newUser: IUser = new User({ name: 'Jack Smith', email: 'jack.smith@example.com' }); await newUser.save();
console.log('New User Saved:', newUser);
}
main()
.catch(error => console.error(error))
.finally(() => mongoose.connection.close());
```

5.2 Running the Application Finally, run your Mongoose setup:

```bash
npx ts-node src/index.ts
```

We explored how to use TypeORM, Prisma, and Mongoose with TypeScript for backend development. Each library offers unique features suited for different projects and developer preferences. Whether you're managing relational data with TypeORM, using a type-

118

safe experience with Prisma, or interacting with documents in MongoDB using Mongoose, TypeScript enhances error handling and developer productivity, making your backend applications cleaner, more maintainable, and easier to scale.

Handling Database Queries and Transactions Efficiently

With TypeScript, developers can leverage strong typing combined with modern JavaScript features to create robust applications that interact with databases effectively. This chapter will cover best practices for writing efficient database queries and managing transactions in TypeScript applications.

1. Understanding the Basics of Database Interaction

Before diving into implementing efficient database queries, it's important to understand the foundational concepts that govern database interactions. Typically, applications communicate with databases through Object-Relational Mapping (ORM) libraries or via raw SQL queries using database drivers.

1.1. Object-Relational Mapping (ORM)

ORMs allow developers to interact with the database using an object-oriented approach, abstracting the complexities of underlying SQL queries. Popular TypeScript-compatible ORMs include:

TypeORM: Provides a powerful, feature-rich experience and supports multiple database systems.

Sequelize: A promise-based ORM for Node.js that

supports various SQL dialects.

Prisma: A modern ORM that focuses on type safety and developer experience.

Typically, ORMs allow for creating, reading, updating, and deleting (CRUD) operations in a more straightforward manner than raw SQL.

1.2. Raw SQL Queries

In scenarios where performance is critical or you need to leverage specific database features, using raw SQL queries may be preferable. TypeScript allows you to access raw queries while maintaining type safety with libraries like `pg-promise` for PostgreSQL or `mysql2` for MySQL.

2. Structuring Database Queries ### 2.1. Use Parameterized Queries

To prevent SQL injection attacks and improve performance, always use parameterized queries when executing SQL commands. Parameterized queries ensure that user input is properly escaped and treated as data, rather than executable code.

```typescript
const getUserById = async (db: Database, userId:
number) => { const query = 'SELECT * FROM users
WHERE id = $1'; const result = await db.query(query,
[userId]);

return result.rows[0];

};
```

2.2. Optimize Your Queries

To make the most of your database interactions, consider the following optimization techniques:

Selective Columns: Only select the fields you need instead of using `SELECT *`. This reduces the amount of data transferred from the database.

```typescript
const getMinimalUserData = async (db: Database, userId: number) => { const query = 'SELECT id, name FROM users WHERE id = $1';

const result = await db.query(query, [userId]); return result.rows[0];

};
```

Indexing: Ensure that the columns most commonly queried against are indexed. This significantly improves query performance.

Batching and Pagination: When dealing with large datasets, use batching and pagination to retrieve only the necessary data.

2.3. Use Connection Pooling

Database connections are expensive to create and destroy. Instead, use a connection pool to maintain a set of active connections that can be reused, improving performance.

```typescript
import { Pool } from 'pg';
```

```typescript
const pool = new Pool({
connectionString: process.env.DATABASE_URL,
});
const getUser = async (userId: number) => {
const result = await pool.query('SELECT * FROM users WHERE id = $1', [userId]); return result.rows[0];
};
```

3. Handling Transactions

Transactions are a fundamental aspect of database interactions, ensuring that a series of operations either all succeed or all fail. This consistency is crucial, especially in multi-step processes.

3.1. Using Transactions

With ORMs or database libraries, transactions can often be managed with dedicated methods. Here's an example using TypeORM:

```typescript
import { getManager } from 'typeorm';

const createUserAndProfile = async (userData: UserData, profileData: ProfileData) => { const entityManager = getManager();

await entityManager.transaction(async (transactionalEntityManager) => { const user = await transactionalEntityManager.save(User, userData); profileData.userId = user.id;
```

```
await          transactionalEntityManager.save(Profile,
profileData);
```

```
});
};
```
```

### 3.2. Error Handling

When working with transactions, ensure proper error handling to maintain data integrity. If any part of the transaction fails, all operations performed during the transaction should be rolled back.

```typescript
try {
await createUserAndProfile(userData, profileData);
} catch (error) {
console.error('Transaction failed, rolling back', error);
// Handle rollback if necessary or just rely on ORM's rollback
}
```

3.3. Leveraging Distributed Transactions

In microservices architectures, you might encounter the need to manage distributed transactions. Consider using Sagas or the Two-Phase Commit protocol to ensure data consistency across services. However, remember that these methods can introduce complexity and should be used judiciously.
```

4. Testing and Performance Monitoring ### 4.1. Unit Testing Database Interactions

When writing unit tests for database interactions, consider using an in-memory database or mocking your database layer. This helps ensure that your tests run quickly and do not require a connection to the actual database.

4.2. Performance Monitoring

Utilize logging and monitoring strategies to keep track of your database queries. Tools like `pino` for logging and APM solutions like New Relic or Datadog can help you identify slow queries or bottlenecks in your application.

Whether you're using an ORM, writing raw SQL, or managing complex transactions, always prioritize security, performance, and maintainability. By adopting these strategies, you can build a robust application that scales smoothly and delivers an exceptional user experience.

Chapter 7: Authentication and Authorization in TypeScript

This chapter dives into how to effectively incorporate these security measures into a TypeScript backend application. We will examine various strategies, libraries, and best practices to ensure data integrity while maintaining a seamless user experience.

7.1 Understanding the Concepts ### 7.1.1 Authentication

Authentication is the process of verifying the identity of a user or system. It is about ensuring that users are who they claim to be. This usually involves users providing credentials, such as a username and password, and validating these against stored records.

7.1.2 Authorization

Authorization, on the other hand, defines what an authenticated user is allowed to do. This might involve permissions related to specific resources, and it usually follows successful authentication. Authorization controls allow system administrators to define roles and permissions for different user groups.

7.2 Setting Up a TypeScript Backend Environment

Before we dive into implementing authentication and authorization, let's set up a basic TypeScript backend environment. We will use Node.js and Express as our server framework. Ensure you have the following prerequisites installed:

Node.js: Both npm and node.js should be available on your machine.

TypeScript: Install TypeScript globally using npm:

```bash
npm install -g typescript
```

Express Framework: Set up a new Express app and TypeScript configuration.

```bash
mkdir my-app cd my-app npm init -y
```

```
npm install express @types/express typescript ts-node --
save-dev
```
` ` `

Create a TypeScript Configuration: Run `tsc --init` to create a `tsconfig.json` file. Now, you have a basic TypeScript setup ready for your backend application.

7.3 Implementing Authentication ### 7.3.1 User Registration and Login

The first step in authentication is to allow users to register and log in. Let's implement this using JSON Web Tokens (JWT) for stateless authentication.

Install Required Packages:

```bash
npm install bcryptjs jsonwebtoken @types/bcryptjs @types/jsonwebtoken
```
` ` `

Create User Model:

Create a `User` model that will represent the user entity in your application.

```typescript
// models/User.ts

import { v4 as uuidv4 } from 'uuid';

export interface User { id: string; username: string;

password: string; // Note: In real apps, avoid storing plain-text passwords
}
```

```typescript
const users: User[] = []; // This will serve as a temporary storage
```

Implement Registration Endpoint:

This endpoint will create a new user. In production, you should use a database instead of an in-memory array.

```typescript
// routes/auth.ts

import express from 'express'; import bcrypt from 'bcryptjs'; import jwt from 'jsonwebtoken';

import { User } from '../models/User'; const router = express.Router();

router.post('/register', async (req, res) => { const { username, password } = req.body;

const hashedPassword = await bcrypt.hash(password, 10);

const newUser: User = { id: uuidv4(), username, password: hashedPassword }; users.push(newUser);

res.status(201).json({ message: 'User registered successfully' });

});
```

Implement Login Endpoint:

This will check user credentials and return a JWT token upon successful verification.

```typescript
router.post('/login', async (req, res) => { const {
username, password } = req.body;

const user = users.find(u => u.username === username);

if (!user || !(await bcrypt.compare(password,
user.password))) { return res.status(401).json({ message:
'Invalid credentials' });
}

const token = jwt.sign({ id: user.id, username:
user.username }, 'your_jwt_secret', { expiresIn: '1h' });
res.json({ token });
});
```

7.3.2 Protecting Routes

To protect our routes and ensure that only authenticated
users can access certain endpoints, we must create
middleware that verifies the JWT token.

```typescript
// middleware/authMiddleware.ts

import { Request, Response, NextFunction } from
'express'; import jwt from 'jsonwebtoken';

export const authenticateJWT = (req: Request, res:
Response, next: NextFunction) => { const token =
req.header('Authorization')?.replace('Bearer ', '');

if (!token) {

return res.sendStatus(401); // Unauthorized
```

```typescript
}
jwt.verify(token, 'your_jwt_secret', (err, user) => { if (err)
{
return res.sendStatus(403); // Forbidden
}
req.user = user; next();
});
};
```

Then, you can apply this middleware to any protected route:

```typescript
router.get('/protected', authenticateJWT, (req, res) => {
res.json({ message: 'This is a protected route', user:
req.user });
});
```

7.4 Implementing Authorization

Once we have authentication in place, we can move on to authorization. A common approach is to define user roles and restrict access based on these roles.

7.4.1 Role-Based Access Control (RBAC)

You may enhance the `User` model to include roles:

```typescript
```

```typescript
export interface User { id: string;
username: string; password: string;
role: string; // e.g., 'admin', 'user', 'editor'
}
```

Then, during registration, admins can assign roles to users. To restrict access based on roles, create a middleware function that checks the user's role:

```typescript
export const authorize = (roles: string[]) => {
return (req: Request, res: Response, next: NextFunction)
=> { const userRole = req.user.role;
if (!roles.includes(userRole)) {
return res.sendStatus(403); // Forbidden
};
};
```

```
}
next();
```

You can now protect a route to allow only admins:

```typescript
router.get('/admin',                     authenticateJWT,
authorize(['admin']), (req, res) => { res.json({ message:
'This is an admin route' });
```

```
});
```
` ` `

7.5 Best Practices

Use HTTPS: Always ensure that your application is served over HTTPS to protect token transmission.

Secure JWTs: Use strong secret keys and consider token expiration times to minimize risks.

Input Validation: Validate user inputs to prevent security vulnerabilities such as SQL injection and XSS.

Logging: Implement logging of authentication attempts and errors for monitoring and incident response.

By leveraging TypeScript with libraries like JWT and bcrypt, you can implement a robust security model in your backend. As applications grow and evolve, continuous updates and attention to security practices will be necessary to protect sensitive information and provide users with a secure experience.

Implementing JWT-Based Authentication in TypeScript

This chapter will walk you through the process of implementing JWT-based authentication in a TypeScript backend. We will cover the essential components including token generation, validation, and securing your API endpoints.

What is JWT?

JSON Web Token (JWT) is a compact, URL-safe means of representing claims to be transferred between two parties. It consists of three parts: a header, a payload, and a signature. This structure allows for the secure transmission of information between a client and a server as it can be verified and trusted.

The general format of a JWT is:

```
eyJhbGciOiJIUzI1NiIsInR5cCI6IkpXVCJ9.eyJzdWIiOiIxM
jMoNTY3ODkwIiwibmFtZSI6IkpvaG4gRG9lIiwiaWWF
```

Prerequisites

Before diving into the implementation, ensure you have the following prerequisites:

Node.js installed on your machine.

A basic understanding of TypeScript.

Familiarity with Express.js or an equivalent framework.

A database (like MongoDB) or an in-memory store for user data (for demonstration). ### Setup

First, let's set up our TypeScript environment. Start by creating a new project folder and initializing a new Node.js project.

```bash
mkdir jwt-auth-example cd jwt-auth-example npm init -y
```

Next, install the required dependencies:

```bash
npm install express jsonwebtoken dotenv bcryptjs cors
npm install --save-dev typescript ts-node @types/node @types/express @types/cors
```

Now, initialize TypeScript configuration:

```bash
npx tsc --init
```

Basic Express Server Setup

Create an `index.ts` file and set up a basic Express server.

```typescript
// src/index.ts

import express from 'express'; import cors from 'cors'; import dotenv from 'dotenv';

dotenv.config();

const app = express(); app.use(cors()); app.use(express.json());

const PORT = process.env.PORT || 3000; app.listen(PORT, () => {

console.log(`Server running on port ${PORT}`);

});
```

Creating User Model

For this example, we need to mimic a user database. Create a basic user interface and some mock users.

```typescript
// src/models/User.ts

interface User { id: number; username: string;

password: string; // In a real app, this should be hashed

}

const users: User[] = [

{

id: 1,

username: 'user1',

password: 'password123' // Note: this should be hashed in production

}

];

export default users;
```

Hashing Passwords

To enhance security, we will use bcrypt.js to hash and compare passwords.

```typescript
// src/utils/auth.ts

import bcrypt from 'bcryptjs';

export const hashPassword = async (password: string) =>
```

```
{ const salt = await bcrypt.genSalt(10);

return await bcrypt.hash(password, salt);

};

export const comparePassword = async (password: string,
hash: string) => { return await bcrypt.compare(password,
hash);

};
```
` ` `

JWT Token Generation

We will create utility functions to generate and verify
JWTs.

` ` `typescript

```
// src/utils/jwt.ts

import jwt from 'jsonwebtoken';

const     secret     =     process.env.JWT_SECRET     ||
'your_jwt_secret'; export const generateToken = (userId:
number) => {

return jwt.sign({ id: userId }, secret, { expiresIn: '1h' });

};

export const verifyToken = (token: string) => { return
jwt.verify(token, secret);

};
```
` ` `

Implementing Authentication Routes

Now, we need to create the authentication routes for user

login that will return a JWT upon a successful login.

```typescript
// src/routes/auth.ts

import express from 'express'; import users from '../models/User';

import { hashPassword, comparePassword } from '../utils/auth'; import { generateToken } from '../utils/jwt';

const router = express.Router(); router.post('/login', async (req, res) => {

const { username, password } = req.body;

const user = users.find(u => u.username === username); if (!user) {

return res.status(404).json({ message: 'User not found' });

}

const isMatch = await comparePassword(password, user.password); if (!isMatch) {

return res.status(401).json({ message: 'Invalid password' });

}

const token = generateToken(user.id); return res.json({ token });

});

export default router;
```

Securing Routes with Middleware

136

To protect our routes, we will create a middleware that validates JWTs.

```typescript
// src/middleware/auth.ts

import { Request, Response, NextFunction } from 'express'; import { verifyToken } from '../utils/jwt';

export const authenticate = (req: Request, res: Response, next: NextFunction) => { const token = req.header('Authorization')?.replace('Bearer ', '');

if (!token) {

return res.status(401).json({ message: 'Access denied' });

}

try {

const verified = verifyToken(token); req.user = verified;

next();

} catch (err) {

res.status(400).json({ message: 'Invalid token' });

}

};
```

Protecting Routes

Finally, apply the middleware to secure a route.

For instance, we want to create a secured route that can only be accessed by authenticated users:

```typescript
```

```typescript
// src/routes/protected.ts
import express from 'express';
import { authenticate } from '../middleware/auth';
const router = express.Router(); router.get('/protected',
authenticate, (req, res) => {
res.json({ message: 'This is a protected route', user:
req.user });

});
export default router;
```

Integrating Everything

In your main `index.ts`, integrate the authentication and protected routes.

```typescript
// src/index.ts
import express from 'express'; import cors from 'cors';
import dotenv from 'dotenv';
import authRoutes from './routes/auth';
import protectedRoutes from './routes/protected';
dotenv.config();
const app = express(); app.use(cors());
app.use(express.json());
app.use('/api/auth', authRoutes); app.use('/api',
protectedRoutes);
```

```
const    PORT    =    process.env.PORT    ||    3000;
app.listen(PORT, () => {

console.log(`Server running on port ${PORT}`);

});
```
```

### Testing Our Implementation

You can now test the implementation using Postman or any API testing tool. Here's a simple way to test:

**Login:**

**Endpoint:** `POST /api/auth/login`

**Body:** `{ "username": "user1", "password": "password123" }`

**Response:** Should return a token if successful.

**Access Protected Route:**

**Endpoint:** `GET /api/protected`

**Headers:** `Authorization: Bearer <your_token>`

**Response:** Should return the protected message if the token is valid.

We covered the implementation of JWT-based authentication in a TypeScript backend. We discussed how to handle user logins, hash passwords for security, generate and validate JWT tokens, and secure API endpoints using middleware. By following these steps, you have laid a strong foundation for implementing authentication in your web applications, enhancing their security and user experience.
```

Role-Based Access Control (RBAC) and OAuth in TypeScript

In this chapter, we will explore the principles of RBAC and OAuth, and how to implement them in a TypeScript-based backend application. This approach not only ensures security and ease of management but also builds a user-friendly experience.

1. Understanding Role-Based Access Control (RBAC)

RBAC is a method of regulating access to computer or network resources based on the roles of individual users within an organization. Users are assigned roles, and each role is associated with permissions that dictate what actions can be performed on specific resources.

1.1 Key Concepts of RBAC

Users: Individual accounts that will interact with the application.

Roles: A grouping of permissions assigned to users. For example, a user with the "Admin" role may have full access to system functionality, whereas a "Viewer" role may have limited access.

Permissions: Specific access rights assigned to roles, allowing or denying actions for resources. ### 1.2 Benefits of RBAC

Improved security: By restricting access based on roles, organizations can minimize the risk of unauthorized access.

Simplicity in user management: Roles streamline the complexity of managing thousands of users by organizing them into manageable groups.

Compliance: Many regulatory standards (such as HIPAA, PCI-DSS) require stringent access controls that can be effectively applied using RBAC.

2. Understanding OAuth

OAuth is an open standard for access delegation, commonly used as a way to grant websites or applications limited access to user information without exposing passwords. It allows applications to securely connect on behalf of a user using access tokens rather than traditional credential passing.

2.1 Key Concepts of OAuth

Resource Owner: The user who authorizes access to their resources.

Client: The application seeking access to the resource owner's data.

Authorization Server: The server that authenticates the resource owner and issues access tokens to the client.

Resource Server: The server that hosts the protected resources and verifies the access tokens. ### 2.2 OAuth Flow

The client requests authorization from the resource owner.

The resource owner grants or denies the request.

If granted, the client receives an authorization grant.

The client exchanges the authorization grant for an access

token at the authorization server.

The client uses the access token to access resources on the resource server.

3. Combining RBAC and OAuth in TypeScript

To implement RBAC and OAuth in a TypeScript backend, we can leverage frameworks such as Express alongside packages like `jsonwebtoken` for handling tokens and `bcrypt` for hashing passwords. Below, we will outline a basic implementation of these concepts.

3.1 Setting Up the Project Install the necessary packages:

```bash
npm install express jsonwebtoken bcrypt @types/express @types/jsonwebtoken @types/bcrypt
```

3.2 Defining User, Role, and Permissions Models

You can define models representing users, roles, and permissions in a TypeScript application.

```typescript
// models/user.ts export interface User {

id: string; username: string; password: string; roleId: string;

}
// models/role.ts export interface Role {

id: string; name: string;

permissions: string[];
```

```typescript
}
```

3.3 Creating Role-Based Access Control Middleware

The following middleware function checks a user's role against the required role for accessing specific routes:

```typescript
import { Request, Response, NextFunction } from "express"; type Role = "Admin" | "Viewer"; // Define roles

const roleMiddleware = (requiredRole: Role) => {

return (req: Request, res: Response, next: NextFunction) => {

const user = req.user; // Assume req.user is populated with authenticated user data

if (user && user.role === requiredRole) { return next();

}

return res.status(403).json({ message: "Forbidden" });

};

};

export default roleMiddleware;
```

3.4 Implementing OAuth Authentication

```typescript
import express from "express"; import jwt from "jsonwebtoken"; import bcrypt from "bcrypt";

import { User } from "./models/user";
```

143

```
const app = express();

const JWT_SECRET = "your_jwt_secret"; // Use
environment variables for security

// Sample users for demonstration. In practice, retrieve
from the database. const users: User[] = [];

app.post("/register", async (req, res) => {

const { username, password, roleId } = req.body;

const hashedPassword = await bcrypt.hash(password, 10);

users.push({ id: Date.now().toString(), username,
password: hashedPassword, roleId });
res.status(201).json({ message: "User registered" });

});

app.post("/login", async (req, res) => { const { username,
password } = req.body;

const user = users.find(u => u.username === username);


if (user && await bcrypt.compare(password,
user.password)) {

const token = jwt.sign({ id: user.id, role: user.roleId },
JWT_SECRET, { expiresIn: "1h" }); return res.json({
token });

}

return res.status(401).json({ message: "Invalid
credentials" });

});

app.get("/protected", roleMiddleware("Admin"), (req, res)
```

```
=> { res.json({ message: "Welcome to the protected route"
});
});
```
```

### 3.5 Token Verification Middleware

To protect routes, add a token verification middleware:

```typescript
const verifyToken = (req: Request, res: Response, next:
NextFunction)      =>      {      const      token      =
req.headers.authorization?.split(" ")[1];

if (!token) return res.status(401).json({ message: "No
token provided" });


jwt.verify(token, JWT_SECRET, (err, decoded) => {

if (err) return res.status(403).json({ message: "Token is
not valid" });

req.user = decoded; next();

});

};

app.use(verifyToken);
```
```

3.6 Testing the Implementation

To test the RBAC and OAuth setup, you can use tools like
Postman:

Register a new user (POST `/register`).

145

Log in to receive a JWT token (POST `/login`).

Use the token to access protected routes (GET `/protected`), ensuring only users with the "Admin" role can access it.

By combining RBAC with OAuth, developers can ensure robust security while maintaining simplicity in user management. Understanding these frameworks not only helps build secure applications but also enhances the overall user experience by providing appropriate access based on user roles.

Chapter 8: Error Handling and Debugging in TypeScript Backend

In this chapter, we will delve into the importance of error handling and debugging in TypeScript for backend development. TypeScript's static type system provides additional tools to manage errors efficiently, enabling developers to build robust applications. We'll explore best practices, common pitfalls, and debugging techniques that can save time and enhance code quality.

8.1 Understanding Errors in TypeScript

In TypeScript, errors can be broadly classified into two categories: compile-time errors and runtime errors. ### 8.1.1 Compile-Time Errors

Compile-time errors are detected by TypeScript's compiler due to type inconsistencies, syntactical mistakes, and violation of type constraints. These errors are advantageous as they can be caught during development before the code is executed, allowing developers to fix issues in real-time.

Example:

```typescript
let username: string = "John";

username = 123; // Compile-time error: Type 'number' is not assignable to type 'string'.
```

8.1.2 Runtime Errors

Runtime errors occur during execution and are typically associated with unexpected conditions in the code, such as

147

accessing a property on an undefined object or throwing an exception. These scenarios can lead to application crashes if not handled properly.

Example:

```typescript
function getUserName(user: { name?: string }) {

return user.name.toUpperCase(); // Runtime error if user.name is undefined.

}
```

Understanding the differences between these two error types is crucial for effectively handling them in your TypeScript backend applications.

8.2 Best Practices for Error Handling

When building a TypeScript backend, it's critical to implement a solid error handling strategy to manage runtime errors gracefully. Here are some best practices:

8.2.1 Use `try-catch` Blocks

`try-catch` blocks allow you to catch errors that may occur during the execution of a particular code block. This approach is especially useful for handling asynchronous calls, such as database queries or API requests.

Example:
```typescript
async function fetchUserProfile(userId: string) { try {

const user = await database.getUserById(userId); return user;

} catch (error) {

console.error('Error fetching user profile:', error);

throw new Error('Could not fetch user profile. Please try again later.');

}

}
```

8.2.2 Custom Error Classes

Creating custom error classes can help you differentiate between error types and provide more context when handling exceptions. You can extend the built-in `Error` class to create specific errors:

```typescript
class NotFoundError extends Error { constructor(message: string) {

super(message);

this.name = "NotFoundError";

}

}
```

When throwing a custom error, you can provide more meaningful messages to the consumer of your API. ### 8.2.3 Error Logging

Implement robust logging mechanisms to record error occurrences. By logging errors, you gather essential information that can help diagnose issues and improve the application's reliability.

8.2.4 Return Error Responses

In a backend application, it's crucial to return appropriate responses to clients when errors occur. Specify HTTP status codes that accurately reflect the error type.

Example:

```typescript
app.get('/user/:id', async (req, res) => { try {

const user = await fetchUserProfile(req.params.id);
res.json(user);

} catch (error) {

if (error instanceof NotFoundError) {
res.status(404).json({ message: error.message });

} else {

res.status(500).json({ message: 'Internal Server Error' });

}

}

});
```

8.3 Debugging Techniques

Effective debugging is vital for diagnosing issues and improving the overall quality of your application. Here are some common techniques to help with debugging TypeScript applications:

8.3.1 Using Console Logging

Utilizing `console.log()` statements can help track the flow of code execution and inspect variable values. While it's a simple method, it's often effective, especially for quick tests.

8.3.2 Using Debuggers

Modern IDEs, like Visual Studio Code, come with built-in debugging tools that facilitate step-through debugging. Set breakpoints, inspect variables, and evaluate expressions to pinpoint issues effectively.

8.3.3 Utilizing Source Maps

When compiling TypeScript, enable source maps to allow debugging in TypeScript rather than the emitted JavaScript. This feature makes it easier to correlate code with errors during execution.

Example Compiler Option:

```json
{
"compilerOptions": { "sourceMap": true
}
}
```

8.3.4 Type Checking and Linting

Employing type checking and linting tools can help catch potential errors early in the development process. Linters like ESLint can enforce coding standards and detect problematic patterns before they become runtime issues.

8.4 Common Pitfalls in Error Handling

Understanding common pitfalls can help avoid errors that may otherwise go unnoticed in the development process:

Overusing Exceptions: Using exceptions for control flow can lead to messy and inefficient code. Reserve exceptions for truly exceptional cases that cannot be handled through regular logic.

Ignoring Error Types: Generic error handling can obscure issues that require specific responses. Be mindful of different error types to provide suitable feedback.

Failing to Log Errors: If errors are not logged, they can go unnoticed, causing frustration for users. Make error logging a standard practice.

By leveraging TypeScript's type system, custom error classes, and robust logging mechanisms, you can create a more resilient application that anticipates and responds to errors effectively. In the absence of a solid error handling strategy, even a small bug can lead to larger repercussions, making knowledge of these concepts indispensable for any backend developer.

Implementing Robust Error Handling Strategies

In a backend environment, especially when using TypeScript, proper error handling allows developers to identify issues early, respond to unexpected situations gracefully, and provide clear feedback to users or downstream services. This chapter will guide you through effective strategies for implementing error handling in TypeScript backend applications, ensuring that your systems are resilient and maintainable.

Understanding Errors in TypeScript

In TypeScript, errors can occur for a variety of reasons, including:

Synchronous Errors: These occur during the execution of code, such as accessing an undefined variable or trying to perform an operation on a null value.

Asynchronous Errors: These happen in asynchronous operations, like handling promises where a rejection occurs, or during network requests.

Logical Errors: These can result from poor logic or unexpected input, leading to incorrect application state or behavior.

To handle these errors effectively, we need to adopt a systematic approach that categorizes them and utilizes TypeScript's strengths, such as strong typing and interfaces.

Establishing a Global Error Handling Strategy

One of the first steps in implementing robust error handling is to create a global error handler. This centralizes error management, making it easier to track and address issues.

Example: Express Middleware for Error Handling

If you are using Express.js, you can create custom middleware to catch errors globally:

```typescript
import { Request, Response, NextFunction } from 'express';

class CustomError extends Error { public statusCode: number;

constructor(message: string, statusCode: number) { super(message);

this.statusCode = statusCode;

}

}

export const errorHandler = (err: CustomError, req: Request, res: Response, next: NextFunction) => { const statusCode = err.statusCode || 500;

const message = err.message || 'Internal Server Error';

res.status(statusCode).json({ status: 'error',

statusCode,


message,

});

};

// Usage in an Express app import express from 'express';
const app = express();

// Other routes and middleware app.use('/api', yourRoutes);
```

154

```typescript
// Global error handling middleware
app.use(errorHandler);
```

In this example, the `CustomError` class extends the native `Error` class to include additional metadata, like

`statusCode`. The global error handler middleware catches errors, makes a response simpler, and ensures consistency across the application.

Handling Asynchronous Errors

As modern applications heavily rely on asynchronous operations (via Promises, async/await, or event-driven architectures), handling errors in these contexts is crucial.

Using Try/Catch with Async/Await

When dealing with async functions, you can utilize `try/catch` blocks to capture errors and forward them to the global handler:

```typescript
import { Request, Response, NextFunction } from 'express';

const yourAsyncFunction = async (req: Request, res: Response, next: NextFunction) => { try {

const data = await someAsyncOperation();
res.status(200).json(data);

} catch (error) {

next(new CustomError('Failed to process request', 500));

}
```

```
};
```

Promises with `.catch()`

While using Promises, you should always attach a `.catch()` method to handle potential rejections:

```typescript
yourAsyncOperation()
```

.then((data) => res.status(200).json(data))

.catch((error) => next(new CustomError('Failed to fetch data', 500)));
```

Implementing these techniques ensures that errors in asynchronous code are also routed to your centralized error handler.

## Categorizing Errors

It's essential to categorize errors for better debugging and user experience. You might have different handling for client errors (status codes 4xx) and server errors (status codes 5xx). For instance, you could set up specific error classes for common types of errors in your application:

### Example of Custom Error Classes

```typescript
class NotFoundError extends CustomError {
constructor(message: string) {
```

super(message, 404);

}

}
```

```typescript
class BadRequestError extends CustomError {
constructor(message: string) {

super(message, 400);

}

}
```

Using these classes, you can easily identify and respond to different types of errors appropriately within your global error handler:

```typescript
export const errorHandler = (err: CustomError, req: Request, res: Response, next: NextFunction) => { if (err instanceof NotFoundError) {

return res.status(err.statusCode).json({ status: 'fail',

message: err.message,

});

}

// Handle other error types...

// Fallback for unknown errors

const statusCode = err.statusCode || 500;

const message = err.message || 'Internal Server Error';
res.status(statusCode).json({

status: 'error', statusCode, message,

});

};
```

```
```

Logging Errors

An effective error handling strategy goes hand-in-hand with logging. Error logs should capture enough context so that developers can diagnose the issue promptly. Use tools like Winston or Morgan for logging:

Example: Using Winston for Logging

```typescript
import { createLogger, format, transports } from 'winston';
const logger = createLogger({ level: 'error',
format: format.combine( format.timestamp(),
format.json()
),
transports: [
new transports.File({ filename: 'error.log' }), new transports.Console()
],
});
export const errorHandler = (err: CustomError, req: Request, res: Response, next: NextFunction) => {
logger.error({
message: err.message, stack: err.stack, method: req.method, url: req.url,
});
// Previous error handling logic...
```

158

```
};
```
` ` `

This will log errors with metadata about the request, making it easier to trace the source of problems.

Implementing robust error handling strategies in TypeScript for backend applications is fundamental to creating resilient, maintainable systems. By establishing a global error handler, categorizing errors, effectively logging them, and handling both synchronous and asynchronous errors, you can create an application that not only responds gracefully to issues but also aids in diagnosing and fixing them swiftly. Embrace these practices, and your backend services will be more robust, reliable, and user-friendly.

Debugging and Logging Techniques for TypeScript Applications

In this chapter, we will explore various debugging techniques and logging practices suited for TypeScript applications in a backend context. The combination of these techniques empowers developers to enhance application performance and maintain a high level of code quality.

Understanding Debugging

Debugging is the process of identifying, isolating, and fixing issues or bugs in software. In TypeScript, debugging can be approached through various means, leveraging the language's features and tools available in the development ecosystem.

Types of Debugging Techniques

Console Logging: The most straightforward form of debugging is using `console.log()`. By inserting print statements in strategic locations within your code, you can observe variable values, execution flow, and function calls.

```typescript
function calculateTotalPrice(items: Item[]): number {
console.log(`Calculating total price for ${items.length} items`); let total = 0;

items.forEach(item => {

console.log(`Item: ${item.name}, Price: ${item.price}`);
total += item.price;

});

return total;

}
```

Interactive Debuggers: Using IDEs with built-in debugging tools (like Visual Studio Code) allows you to set breakpoints, step through code, and inspect variable states interactively. This can dramatically speed up the debugging process.

Setting Breakpoints: Stop the execution of your application at specific lines of code.

Inspect Variables: Check the values of variables at various points during execution.

TypeScript Compiler Options: Leverage TypeScript's

compiler options such as `sourceMap`. This feature allows you to debug TypeScript code directly in the browser or IDE, making it easier to trace errors back to their TypeScript source rather than compiled JavaScript.

```json
{
"compilerOptions": { "sourceMap": true, "outDir": "./dist",
"strict": true
}
}
```

Error Handling with Try...Catch: Use `try...catch` blocks to gracefully handle errors and gather insights on what went wrong.

```typescript
async function fetchData(url: string) { try {
const response = await fetch(url);
if (!response.ok) throw new Error("Network response was not ok"); const data = await response.json();
return data;
} catch (error) {
console.error('Fetch Error:', error);
}
}
```

161

Unit Testing: Incorporate robust unit testing in your development workflow with frameworks like Jest or Mocha. Tests can help identify bugs early by ensuring that individual components work as expected.

```typescript
describe("calculateTotalPrice", () => {

it("should return the correct total price", () => {

const items = [{ name: "item1", price: 10 }, { name: "item2", price: 20 }];
expect(calculateTotalPrice(items)).toBe(30);

});

});
```

Effective Logging Techniques

Logging is crucial for monitoring the behavior of your application in a production environment. A well-structured logging system can provide actionable insights for identifying bottlenecks and debugging production issues.

Core Principles of Logging

Log Levels: Use different log levels (e.g., DEBUG, INFO, WARN, ERROR) to categorize logs, making them easier to filter and analyze.

DEBUG: Detailed information used for diagnostics.

INFO: General operational messages.

WARN: Indications of potential issues.

ERROR: Runtime errors and exceptions.

```typescript
import { createLogger, transports, format } from 'winston';
const logger = createLogger({ level: 'info',
format: format.combine( format.timestamp(),
format.json()
),
transports: [
new transports.Console(),
new transports.File({ filename: 'error.log', level: 'error' }),
new transports.File({ filename: 'combined.log' }),
],
});
```

Structured Logging: Use structured logging formats (like JSON) to enable better parsing and filtering of log data.

```typescript
logger.info('UserLogin', { userId: 123, timestamp: new Date() });
```

Centralized Logging: Implement centralized logging solutions (like ELK Stack, Splunk, or broader cloud services like AWS CloudWatch) to aggregate logs in one place for better analysis and monitoring.

Correlation IDs: In microservices architecture, use correlation IDs to track requests across multiple services, providing a holistic view of a request's lifecycle.

```typescript
import { v4 as uuidv4 } from 'uuid';

const correlationId = uuidv4();

logger.info('Request received', { correlationId, path: '/api/v1/resource' });
```

Best Practices for Debugging and Logging

Don't Depend Solely on Console Logs: While console logging can be helpful during development, it should not be relied upon for production applications because it doesn't provide the richness and features of proper logging frameworks.

Log Meaningful Messages: Ensure that your log messages are clear and informative. They should provide context to help understand what condition led to the log entry.

Monitor Application Health: Use tools like application performance monitoring (APM) to visualize application metrics and logs in real-time. This can help detect anomalies before they escalate into larger problems.

Regularly Review and Refactor Logs: As your application evolves, the relevance of logs may change. Regularly audit and refactor your logging strategy to ensure it meets current needs.

Protect Sensitive Data: Be mindful of security and privacy concerns when logging. Ensure that sensitive information (like passwords or personal data) is never logged.

By employing a combination of effective debugging techniques and structured logging practices, developers can not only resolve issues more efficiently but also create a system that is robust, maintainable, and easier to understand. A conscientious approach to these practices will ultimately lead to higher quality applications and more satisfied users.

Chapter 9: Writing Clean, Maintainable, and Scalable Code

TypeScript, a superset of JavaScript that incorporates static typing, offers a robust foundation for creating high-quality code. In this chapter, we will explore key principles and best practices for writing clean, maintainable, and scalable code in TypeScript for backend applications.

1. Understanding Clean Code Principles

Clean code is characterized by readability, simplicity, and minimalism. It follows guidelines that make it easier for developers to understand and modify the codebase. Some of the primary principles of clean code include:

1.1 Descriptive Naming

Variable, function, and class names should be descriptive enough to convey their purpose. Avoid abbreviations and generic names. For example, instead of naming a user retrieval function `getUser`, a name like `fetchUserById` clearly indicates the method's specific action.

```typescript
// Clean

function fetchUserById(userId: string): User { /* implementation */ }

// Not Clean

function gU(userId: string) { /* implementation */ }
```

1.2 Function Size and Single Responsibility

Each function should perform a single task. When

functions grow too large or handle multiple responsibilities, they become difficult to read and maintain. If a function exceeds 20 lines or performs multiple operations, consider refactoring it.

```typescript
// Single Responsibility
function saveUser(user: User): void { /* Save Logic */ }

function sendWelcomeEmail(user: User): void { /* Email Logic */ }
```

1.3 Proper Use of Comments

While code should be self-explanatory, comments can add value when explaining the why behind complex logic. However, avoid redundant comments that explain the obvious. They can make the code cluttered and harder to read.

```typescript
// Clean
if (!userExists) {

throw new Error('User does not exist'); // Reason why we throw an error

}
// Not Clean
// Check if user exists if (!userExists) {

throw new Error('User does not exist');

}
```

167

```
```

2. Maintainability Through Architecture

A maintainable codebase allows developers to easily update and extend functionality without introducing bugs. Several architectural patterns help achieve maintainability:

2.1 Modular Architecture

Break your application into modules or services. Each module should ideally encapsulate a specific feature or logical entity, such as authentication or data processing.

```typescript
// User Module

export class UserService {

createUser(userData: UserDto) { /* implementation */ }

}

export class UserController {

createUser(req: Request, res: Response) { /* implementation */ }

}
```

2.2 Dependency Injection

Use Dependency Injection (DI) to manage dependencies. It facilitates easier testing and promotes loose coupling between classes.

```typescript
class UserService {
```

```typescript
  constructor(private userRepository: UserRepository) {}
  findUser(id: string): User { /* implementation */ }
}
```

2.3 Consistent Structure with MVC

Using the Model-View-Controller (MVC) pattern or similar structures can help maintain a clear separation of concerns, especially in larger projects.

```typescript
// MVC Structure

class UserModel { /* Model Logic */ }

class UserController { /* Controller Logic */ } class UserView { /* View Logic */ }
```

3. Scaling Up with TypeScript

As applications grow, so do the complexities involved. Writing scalable code involves anticipating future changes and potential issues.

3.1 Type Safety

TypeScript's static typing helps catch errors early. Use interfaces and types extensively to define the shape of objects and ensure your code remains type-safe.

```typescript
interface User {
  id: string; name: string;
}
// Type-safe function signature
```

```typescript
function getUserName(user: User): string { return user.name;
}
```

3.2 Asynchronous Programming

Leverage asynchronous patterns—like Promises and `async/await`—to handle I/O operations efficiently. This is crucial in a backend context where numerous tasks may occur concurrently.

```typescript
async function fetchData(): Promise<Data> { const response = await fetch('/api/data'); return response.json();
}
```

3.3 Event-Driven Architecture

For large applications, consider using an event-driven architecture, where components communicate through events. This reduces tight coupling and increases scalability.

```typescript
import { EventEmitter } from 'events';

const eventEmitter = new EventEmitter();
eventEmitter.on('userCreated', (user: User) => {

// Handle user creation logic

});
```

```
```

4. Testing and Documentation

A clean, maintainable codebase is ineffective if it is not tested or documented. ### 4.1 Test-Driven Development (TDD)

Adopt TDD practices to ensure your code is well-tested from the start. Writing tests alongside your implementation can help prevent regressions.

```typescript
describe('UserService', () => {

it('should create a user successfully', () => { const userService = new UserService();

const user = userService.createUser({ /* Mock Data */ });
expect(user).toBeDefined();

});

});
```

4.2 Documentation

Use tools like TypeDoc to generate documentation from your TypeScript code. Ensure that complex pieces of logic and APIs are well-documented for future developers.

```typescript

/**

Fetch a user by ID

@param userId - ID of the user to fetch

@returns The user object
```

```
*/
function fetchUserById(userId: string): User { /*
implementation */ }
```
` ` `

By adhering to the principles outlined in this chapter—such as descriptive naming, single responsibility, proper structuring, and ensuring type safety—you will position your code for long-term maintainability and adaptability.

Following SOLID Principles and Design Patterns in TypeScript

One effective way to achieve this is by adhering to the SOLID principles and utilizing design patterns. While these concepts are language-agnostic, they can be particularly effective when applied within a TypeScript context, especially for backend development. This chapter delves into the SOLID principles, introduces common design patterns, and demonstrates their application in TypeScript to enhance backend architecture.

Understanding SOLID Principles

The SOLID principles are a set of five design principles that aim to make software designs more understandable, flexible, and maintainable. The acronym stands for:

S - Single Responsibility Principle (SRP)

O - Open/Closed Principle (OCP)

L - Liskov Substitution Principle (LSP)

I - Interface Segregation Principle (ISP)

D - Dependency Inversion Principle (DIP) ### Single Responsibility Principle (SRP)

The SRP states that a class should have only one reason to change, meaning it should have only one job or responsibility. In the context of a backend application, this could mean separating concerns such as routing, data access, and business logic into distinct modules or services.

Example in TypeScript:

```typescript
// UserService.ts class UserService {
constructor(private userRepository: UserRepository) {}
public registerUser(userData: UserDTO) {
// Registration logic
}
public getUser(userId: string) {
return this.userRepository.findById(userId);
}
}
// UserRepository.ts class UserRepository {
private users: User[] = [];
public findById(userId: string): User | null {
return this.users.find(user => user.id === userId) || null;
}
```

173

```
}
```
```

```

Open/Closed Principle (OCP)

The OCP states that software entities should be open for extension but closed for modification. This principle encourages developers to write code that can be extended without changing existing code.

Example in TypeScript:

```typescript
abstract class Notification {

abstract send(message: string): void;

}

class EmailNotification extends Notification {
send(message: string) {

console.log(`Sending email: ${message}`);

}

}

class SmsNotification extends Notification {
send(message: string) {

console.log(`Sending SMS: ${message}`);

}

}

class NotificationService {

constructor(private notification: Notification) {}

notify(message: string) { this.notification.send(message);
```

```
}
}
```

Liskov Substitution Principle (LSP)

The LSP posits that objects of a superclass should be replaceable with objects of a subclass without affecting the correctness of the program. This principle is especially significant in ensuring type safety in TypeScript.

Example in TypeScript:

```typescript
class Square {
constructor(private side: number) {}

public area(): number { return this.side * this.side;
}
}
class Rectangle {
constructor(private width: number, private height: number) {}

public area(): number {

return this.width * this.height;


}
}
// Ensure both can be used interchangeably function printArea(shape: { area: () => number }) {

console.log(`Area: ${shape.area()}`);
```

```
}
```

const square = new Square(5);

const rectangle = new Rectangle(5, 10);

printArea(square); printArea(rectangle);

``` ` ` ` ```

Interface Segregation Principle (ISP)

The ISP suggests that no client should be forced to depend on methods it does not use. This principle advocates for smaller and more focused interfaces.

Example in TypeScript:

``` ` ` `typescript ```

```typescript
interface UserManagement { createUser(user: User): void;
deleteUser(userId: string): void;

}

interface OrderManagement { createOrder(order: Order):
void; cancelOrder(orderId: string): void;

}

class UserService implements UserManagement {
createUser(user: User) { /* implementation */ }
deleteUser(userId: string) { /* implementation */ }

}

class OrderService implements OrderManagement {
createOrder(order: Order) { /* implementation */ }
cancelOrder(orderId: string) { /* implementation */ }

}
```
``` ` ` ` ```
```

Dependency Inversion Principle (DIP)

The DIP emphasizes that high-level modules should not depend on low-level modules but rather both should depend on abstractions. For TypeScript, this can be achieved through the use of interfaces and dependency injection.

Example in TypeScript:

```typescript
interface ILogger {

log(message: string): void;

}

class ConsoleLogger implements ILogger { log(message: string) {

console.log(message);

}

}

class UserService {

constructor(private logger: ILogger) {}

public register(user: User) { this.logger.log('Registering user...');

// Registration logic

}

}
```

Design Patterns in TypeScript

Design patterns are tried and tested solutions to common

problems in software design. Understanding these patterns can aid in creating a more structured and efficient codebase. Here we will explore some common design patterns relevant to backend development.

Singleton Pattern

The Singleton Pattern ensures a class has only one instance and provides a global point of access to it. This is particularly useful for logging services or database connections.

Example in TypeScript:

```typescript
class DatabaseConnection {

private static instance: DatabaseConnection;

private constructor() { /* Initialization logic */ } public static getInstance(): DatabaseConnection {

if (!DatabaseConnection.instance) { DatabaseConnection.instance = new DatabaseConnection();

}

return DatabaseConnection.instance;

}

}
```

Factory Pattern

The Factory Pattern provides a way to create objects without specifying the exact class of the object that will be created. It promotes loose coupling and scalability.

Example in TypeScript:

```typescript
typescript interface User {
name: string;
}
class AdminUser implements User { constructor(public name: string) {}
}
class RegularUser implements User { constructor(public name: string) {}
}
class UserFactory {
static createUser(type: 'admin' | 'regular', name: string): User { switch (type) {
case 'admin':
return new AdminUser(name); case 'regular':
return new RegularUser(name);
}
}
}
```

Repository Pattern

The Repository Pattern abstracts the data access layer,

promoting a clean separation between the domain logic and data access code. This pattern is particularly useful in applications that require a clear data management strategy.

Example in TypeScript:

```typescript
interface IUserRepository { findAll(): User[];

findById(id: string): User | null;

}

class UserRepository implements IUserRepository {
private users: User[] = [];

findAll(): User[] { return this.users;

}

findById(id: string): User | null {

return this.users.find(user => user.id === id) || null;

}

}

```

By emphasizing separation of concerns, extensibility, and robust architecture, developers can create systems that are easier to manage, adapt, and extend. As the complexity of applications grows, embracing these principles and patterns will pave the way for cleaner, more dependable code, ultimately leading to better software solutions.

Modularizing Code and Using Dependency Injection

In the context of backend development with TypeScript, two essential practices stand out: modularizing code and utilizing Dependency Injection (DI). This chapter delves into these concepts, illustrating their significance and providing practical examples to help you implement them effectively in your TypeScript applications.

1. Why Modularize Code?

1.1 Benefits of Modularization

Modularization involves breaking down an application into smaller, manageable pieces or modules. This practice brings several benefits:

Separation of Concerns: Each module can focus on a distinct functionality, making it easier to understand and maintain.

Reusability: Modules can be reused across different parts of the application or even across different projects.

Testability: Smaller modules can be tested independently, enhancing the overall test coverage and reliability of the application.

Collaboration: Multiple developers can work on different modules simultaneously without causing conflicts in code, fostering a more collaborative environment.

1.2 Structure of a Modularized Application

In a modularized TypeScript application, it is common to

organize code into folders based on functionality. A typical directory structure might look like this:

```
` ` `

/src

/controllers

/models

/services

/routes

/middlewares

/utils

/config index.ts

` ` `
```

Each folder contains files that serve specific purposes related to the application's functionality. For instance, the `controllers` folder may contain files that handle incoming requests, while the `models` folder contains definitions for database entities.

2. Implementing Modular Code in TypeScript

Let's explore a simple example of how to modularize a TypeScript application. Below, we'll create a basic user management system.

2.1 User Model

Create a file named `User.ts` in the `models` folder.

```typescript
// src/models/User.ts export class User {
```

```typescript
constructor(public id: number, public name: string, public email: string) {}
}
```

2.2 User Service

Next, create a service that contains the business logic related to users. Save this as `UserService.ts` in the `services` folder.

```typescript
// src/services/UserService.ts

import { User } from '../models/User';

export class UserService { private users: User[] = [];

public addUser(name: string, email: string): User {

const user = new User(this.users.length + 1, name, email);
this.users.push(user);

return user;

}

public getAllUsers(): User[] { return this.users;

}
}
```

2.3 User Controller

Create a controller to handle HTTP requests related to users. This will be saved as `UserController.ts` in the `controllers` folder.

```typescript
// src/controllers/UserController.ts

import { UserService } from '../services/UserService';
import { Request, Response } from 'express';

export class UserController {

constructor(private userService: UserService) {}

public addUser(req: Request, res: Response): void { const
{ name, email } = req.body;

const user = this.userService.addUser(name, email);
res.status(201).json(user);

}

public getAllUsers(req: Request, res: Response): void {
const users = this.userService.getAllUsers();
res.status(200).json(users);

}

}
```

2.4 Setting Up Routes

Now, set up routes to map HTTP requests to the corresponding controller actions. Create a file named

`userRoutes.ts` in the `routes` folder.

```typescript
// src/routes/userRoutes.ts import { Router } from
'express';
```

184

```typescript
import { UserService } from '../services/UserService';
import { UserController } from '../controllers/UserController';
const userService = new UserService();
const userController = new UserController(userService);
const router = Router();
router.post('/users', (req, res) => userController.addUser(req, res)); router.get('/users', (req, res) => userController.getAllUsers(req, res));
export default router;
```

2.5 Main Application Entry Point

Finally, let's tie everything together in `index.ts` in the `src` folder.

```typescript
// src/index.ts
import express from 'express';
import userRoutes from './routes/userRoutes';
const app = express(); app.use(express.json());
app.use('/api', userRoutes);
const PORT = process.env.PORT || 3000; app.listen(PORT, () => {
console.log(`Server is running on port ${PORT}`);
});
```

3. Understanding Dependency Injection ### 3.1 What is Dependency Injection?

Dependency Injection (DI) is a design pattern that allows a class to receive its dependencies from an external source rather than instantiating them directly. This promotes loose coupling, easier testing, and better maintainability.

3.2 Benefits of Dependency Injection

Improved Testability: You can easily mock dependencies while testing a class, leading to more effective unit tests.

Decoupling: Reduces the dependency between components, providing greater flexibility.

Enhanced Maintainability: Changes to a dependency require minimal changes to the dependent classes.

3.3 Implementing Dependency Injection in TypeScript

In the example above, the `UserController` class relies on the `UserService` class. Instead of the controller creating an instance of the service internally, we passed it as a constructor argument, facilitating Dependency Injection.

However, without a DI container, managing dependencies can become cumbersome in larger applications. For more extensive applications, you might consider using a DI framework, such as `InversifyJS`.

3.4 Using InversifyJS for Dependency Injection

Install InversifyJS:

```bash
npm install inversify reflect-metadata
```

```
` ` `
```

Add Decorators:

Ensure your TypeScript configuration allows decorators by adding the following to your `tsconfig.json`:

```json
{
"experimentalDecorators":                    true,
"emitDecoratorMetadata": true
}
```

Configure InversifyJS:

Modify your service and controller to use InversifyJS decorators.

```typescript
// src/services/UserService.ts

import { injectable } from 'inversify'; import { User } from '../models/User';

@injectable()

export class UserService { private users: User[] = [];

public addUser(name: string, email: string): User {

const user = new User(this.users.length + 1, name, email); this.users.push(user);

return user;
}

public getAllUsers(): User[] { return this.users;
```

```typescript
  }
}
// src/controllers/UserController.ts
import { inject, injectable } from 'inversify';

import { UserService } from '../services/UserService';
import { Request, Response } from 'express';

@injectable()

export class UserController {

constructor(@inject(UserService) private userService: UserService) {}

public addUser(req: Request, res: Response): void { const { name, email } = req.body;

const user = this.userService.addUser(name, email);
res.status(201).json(user);

}

public getAllUsers(req: Request, res: Response): void {
const users = this.userService.getAllUsers();
res.status(200).json(users);

}

}
```

Create a Container:

In your `index.ts`, create an InversifyJS container to manage dependency resolutions.

```typescript
```

```typescript
// src/index.ts
import 'reflect-metadata'; // Import as the first line
import express from 'express';

import { Container } from 'inversify';

import userRoutes from './routes/userRoutes';

import { UserService } from './services/UserService';

import { UserController } from './controllers/UserController';

const app = express(); app.use(express.json());

const container = new Container();
container.bind<UserService>(UserService).toSelf();
container.bind<UserController>(UserController).toSelf();

// Create an instance of the UserController through the container

const userController = container.get<UserController>(UserController);
app.post('/users', (req, res) => userController.addUser(req, res)); app.get('/users', (req, res) => userController.getAllUsers(req, res));


const PORT = process.env.PORT || 3000;
app.listen(PORT, () => {

console.log(`Server is running on port ${PORT}`);

});
```

By organizing code into modular components, you

189

promote better maintainability and scalability, while DI enhances testability and decouples dependencies. By following the examples and guidelines discussed in this chapter, you can effectively create robust, modular, and easy-to-maintain backend applications in TypeScript.

Chapter 10: Asynchronous Programming with TypeScript

With the ever-increasing demand for responsive applications that can handle multiple tasks concurrently, mastering asynchronous programming has become more important than ever. This chapter will guide you through the foundational concepts, various patterns, and practical implementations of asynchronous code in a TypeScript backend.

10.1 Understanding Asynchronous Programming

Asynchronous programming allows you to execute long-running tasks without blocking the execution of the main code. In a traditional synchronous approach, the program waits for a task to complete before moving on to the next line of code. This can be inefficient, especially for I/O-bound tasks such as network requests, file operations, and database queries, where the program would otherwise sit idle, waiting.

In contrast, asynchronous programming enables the execution of other code while these tasks are pending. This results in more efficient use of resources, improved performance, and better user experiences, especially in web applications.

10.1.1 Callbacks

The simplest form of asynchronous programming is the use of callbacks. In this pattern, you pass a function (callback) as an argument to another function, which is then executed once an async operation completes.

Example:

```typescript
function fetchData(callback: (data: string) => void) {
setTimeout(() => {
// Simulates a network request callback('Data received');
}, 1000);
}
fetchData((data) => {
console.log(data); // Output: Data received
});
```

While callbacks are straightforward, they can lead to "callback hell," where nested callbacks make the code difficult to read and maintain.

10.1.2 Promises

To overcome the limitations of callbacks, JavaScript introduced Promises. A Promise represents a value that may be available now, or in the future, or never. Promises provide a cleaner and more manageable way to handle asynchronous operations.

Example:

```typescript
function fetchData(): Promise<string> {
return new Promise((resolve) => { setTimeout(() => {
resolve('Data received');
}, 1000);
```

```
});
}
fetchData().then((data) => { console.log(data); // Output:
Data received
});
```

In this example, `fetchData()` returns a Promise that resolves after 1 second. You can chain `.then()` to handle the result, leading to more readable code.

10.1.3 Async/Await

Introduced in ES2017, `async` and `await` provide a more elegant syntax for working with Promises. An `async` function returns a Promise, and `await` pauses the execution of the function until the Promise is resolved.

Example:

```typescript
async function fetchData(): Promise<string> { return new
Promise((resolve) => {

setTimeout(() => { resolve('Data received');

}, 1000);

});
}
async function main() {

const data = await fetchData(); console.log(data); //
Output: Data received
```

```
}
main();
```
```` ``` ````

With `async/await`, the code appears synchronous while still being non-blocking, making it easier to read and maintain.

10.2 Error Handling

When working with asynchronous code, especially in a backend context, handling errors gracefully is pivotal. Promises provide a `.catch()` method to handle rejections, while `async/await` uses `try/catch` blocks for error handling.

Example:

```typescript
async function fetchData(): Promise<string> { return new Promise((resolve, reject) => {

setTimeout(() => {

reject(new Error('Failed to fetch data'));


}, 1000);
});
}
async function main() { try {
const data = await fetchData(); console.log(data);
} catch (error) {
```
```

```
console.error(error.message);  // Output: Failed to fetch
data
}
}
main();
```

By implementing proper error handling, you can ensure that your application remains robust and can recover from failures effectively.

10.3 Practical Implementation: Building a REST API

Let's take a practical approach by building a simple REST API using TypeScript with asynchronous programming. We will use Express, a popular web framework, to create this API.

10.3.1 Setting Up the Project

First, we need to set up a new TypeScript project. You can do this by running the following commands:

```bash
mkdir ts-async-api cd ts-async-api npm init -y

npm install express @types/express typescript ts-node --save-dev npx tsc --init
```

10.3.2 Creating the Server

Now let's create a basic Express server with asynchronous routes.

```typescript
```

```typescript
// server.ts
import express, { Request, Response } from 'express';
const app = express(); const port = 3000;
// Middleware to parse JSON app.use(express.json());
// Fake database
const users: Array<{ id: number; name: string }> = [];
// Async route to create a user
app.post('/users', async (req: Request, res: Response) => {
const { name } = req.body;
const userId = users.length + 1;
// Simulating a database operation
await new Promise((resolve) => setTimeout(resolve, 500));
users.push({ id: userId, name }); res.status(201).json({ id: userId, name });
});
// Async route to get all users
app.get('/users', async (req: Request, res: Response) => {
// Simulating a database operation
await new Promise((resolve) => setTimeout(resolve, 500));
res.json(users);
});
// Starting the server app.listen(port, () => {
```

```
console.log(`Server running at http://localhost:${port}`);
});
```

10.3.3 Testing the API

You can test the API using tools like Postman or curl. Here are example commands:

- **Create a User**:

```bash
curl -X POST http://localhost:3000/users -H "Content-Type: application/json" -d '{"name": "John Doe"}'
```

- **Get All Users**:

```bash
curl http://localhost:3000/users
```

In this chapter, we covered the basics of callbacks, Promises, and the async/await syntax, along with practical implementations in the context of a REST API. With these tools in your toolkit, you can handle I/O-bound tasks efficiently, ensuring that your applications remain responsive and deliver a positive user experience.

Understanding Async/Await, Promises, and Event Loop

Understanding how async/await, promises, and the event loop function together is crucial for building responsive and performant applications. In this chapter, we will delve deep into these concepts, showcasing practical examples in TypeScript to solidify your understanding.

1. Asynchronous Programming: An Overview

Asynchronous programming allows your code to run without blocking the execution thread. This is particularly important in a backend environment where tasks such as database queries, file operations, or network requests can take a considerable amount of time to complete. Instead of waiting for these tasks to finish, asynchronous programming enables your application to handle other operations, improving overall responsiveness and throughput.

1.1 The Need for Asynchronous Programming

Consider a scenario where your server handles an HTTP request to fetch user data from a database. If you execute this task synchronously, the server will halt all other operations, ultimately leading to sluggish performance or unresponsiveness. Asynchronous programming helps mitigate this by allowing other requests to be processed while waiting for the database operation to complete.

2. Promises: The Foundation of Asynchronous Control Flow

Promises are a fundamental building block of

asynchronous JavaScript. A promise represents an operation that hasn't completed yet but is expected to in the future. They can be in one of three states: pending, fulfilled, or rejected.

2.1 Creating Promises

In TypeScript, creating a promise is straightforward. Here's a simple example of a promise that simulates fetching user data from a database:

```typescript
function fetchUserData(userId: string): Promise<{ id: string; name: string }> { return new Promise((resolve, reject) => {

setTimeout(() => { if (userId) {

resolve({ id: userId, name: 'John Doe' });

} else {

reject(new Error('User ID is required'));

}

}, 2000);

});

}
```

2.2 Consuming Promises

You can handle the results of a promise using the `.then()` and `.catch()` methods:

```typescript
fetchUserData('123')

.then(user => {
```

```
console.log('User Data:', user);
})
.catch(error => {
console.error('Error fetching user data:', error);
});
```
` ` `

2.3 Chaining Promises

Promises can be chained together to perform a series of asynchronous operations. Each `.then()` returns a new promise. For instance:

```typescript
fetchUserData('123')
.then(user => {
return fetchUserPosts(user.id); // Assume this also returns a Promise
})
.then(posts => {
console.log('User Posts:', posts);
})
.catch(error => { console.error('Error:', error);
});
```
` ` `

3. Async/Await: Syntactical Sugar Over Promises

Async/await is syntactic sugar built on top of promises, allowing for more readable and straightforward code. It helps reduce the complexity associated with chaining multiple promises.

3.1 Using Async/Await

To use async/await, you simply prefix your function with the `async` keyword. Inside this function, you can now use the `await` keyword to pause the execution of the function until the promise is resolved. Here's how it looks:

```typescript
async function displayUserData(userId: string) { try {

const user = await fetchUserData(userId); console.log('User Data:', user);

const posts = await fetchUserPosts(user.id); // Assume this also returns a Promise console.log('User Posts:', posts);

} catch (error) { console.error('Error:', error);

}

}
```

3.2 Error Handling

Error handling with async/await is typically done using `try/catch` blocks, making it feel more intuitive compared to promise chains.

3.3 Parallel Execution

While `await` pauses the execution, there are scenarios where you may want to execute multiple asynchronous tasks in parallel. You can achieve this using

`Promise.all()`:

```typescript
async function displayUserAndPosts(userId: string) { try {
const userPromise = fetchUserData(userId);
const postsPromise = fetchUserPosts(userId); // Assume this also returns a Promise const [user, posts] = await Promise.all([userPromise, postsPromise]);

console.log('User Data:', user); console.log('User Posts:', posts);
} catch (error) { console.error('Error:', error);
}
}
```

4. The Event Loop: The Heart of Asynchronous JavaScript

Understanding the event loop is key to mastering asynchronous programming in JavaScript and TypeScript. The event loop is a single-threaded mechanism that allows JavaScript to perform non-blocking operations.

4.1 How the Event Loop Works

Call Stack: This is where your code is executed. When a function is called, it gets pushed to the call stack and executed. Upon completion, it is popped off the stack.

Web APIs: When an asynchronous function is invoked

(like `setTimeout`, `fetch`, etc.), the execution is handed off to the browser's Web API, which runs outside the call stack.

Callback Queue: Once an asynchronous operation completes, its callback (or the code associated with it) moves to the callback queue.

Event Loop: The event loop constantly checks the call stack. If the call stack is empty and there are items in the callback queue, the event loop will dequeue and execute them.

4.2 Example of the Event Loop in Action

```typescript
console.log('Start');

setTimeout(() => { console.log('Timeout callback');
}, 0);

fetchUserData('456').then(user => { console.log('Fetched user:', user);
});


console.log('End');
```

Expected Output:

```
Start End

Fetched user: { id: '456', name: 'John Doe' } Timeout callback
```

By understanding async/await, promises, and the event

loop, you gain a powerful toolkit for handling asynchronous operations in your TypeScript backend applications. These tools not only help in writing efficient code but also enhance the readability and maintainability of your codebase.

Optimizing Performance with Worker Threads and Queues

In this chapter, we will explore how to leverage Worker Threads and queues in TypeScript to enhance the performance of Node.js applications. We will begin with an overview of Worker Threads, delve into how to implement them in a TypeScript backend, and finally discuss the role of queues in task management.

Understanding Worker Threads

Worker Threads are a solution to achieve multithreading in Node.js, allowing CPU-intensive tasks to run in parallel without blocking the main thread. This improvement is essential, especially in applications requiring heavy computations. The Worker Threads module provides a way to execute JavaScript in parallel on separate threads.

Key Benefits

Non-blocking: Offload heavy computations to worker threads to keep the main thread responsive.

Concurrency: Facilitate the execution of multiple tasks simultaneously, enhancing throughput.

Separation of Concerns: Isolate different parts of the application, making it easier to manage complex logic.

Setting Up Worker Threads in TypeScript ### Prerequisites

Ensure that you have Node.js installed (version 10.5.0 or later). You will also need TypeScript and the

`@types/node` package for type definitions.

Install TypeScript:

```bash
npm install typescript --save-dev
```

Install the Node.js type definitions:

```bash
npm install @types/node --save-dev
```

Creating a Worker

Below is a straightforward example of how to create a worker thread in TypeScript:

First, create a new directory structure for your project.

```
/project package.json tsconfig.json


index.ts worker.ts
```

In `worker.ts`, implement the logic you want to execute in the worker thread.

```typescript
// worker.ts
import { parentPort } from 'worker_threads';
parentPort?.on('message', (data) => {
const result = data.value * 2; // Example computation
parentPort?.postMessage({ result });
});
```

In `index.ts`, create and manage the worker.

```typescript
// index.ts
import { Worker } from 'worker_threads'; import path from 'path';

function runService(data: any): Promise<any> { return new Promise((resolve, reject) => {

const worker = new Worker(path.resolve(__dirname, 'worker.ts')); worker.postMessage(data);

worker.on('message', (message) => { resolve(message);
});
worker.on('error', (error) => { reject(error);
});
worker.on('exit', (code) => { if (code !== 0) {

reject(new Error(`Worker stopped with exit code ${code}`));
}
```

```
});
});
}
(async () => { try {
```

const result = await runService({ value: 4 });
console.log(result); // Output: { result: 8 }

```
} catch (error) { console.error(error);
}
})();
```
```

### Executing the Code

To execute the code, compile the TypeScript files to JavaScript and run the output:

```bash npx tsc
node index.js
```

You should see the output confirming the operation processed in the worker. ## Implementing Queues for Task Management

Worker Threads shine in an environment where tasks can be queued, allowing multiple computations to be dispatched without overwhelming the system. For this purpose, using a queue system can significantly improve concurrency management.

Integrating a Queue

For our example, we'll use a simple array-based queue.
```

However, for production-level applications, consider using libraries like Bull or Bee-Queue for more robust functionality.

Create a queue class to manage tasks.

```typescript
// queue.ts
class TaskQueue {
  private tasks: (() => Promise<any>)[] = []; private
  activeWorkers: number = 0; private maxWorkers:
  number;

  constructor(maxWorkers: number) { this.maxWorkers =
  maxWorkers;
  }

  public addTask(task: () => Promise<any>) {
  this.tasks.push(task);

  this.runNext();
  }

  private async runNext() {

  if (this.activeWorkers < this.maxWorkers &&
  this.tasks.length > 0) { this.activeWorkers++;

  const currentTask = this.tasks.shift(); if (currentTask) {

  await currentTask();

  }

  this.activeWorkers--; this.runNext();

  }
```

```typescript
  }
}
export default TaskQueue;
```

Modify your worker and index files to utilize the queue.

```typescript
// index.ts updated

import TaskQueue from './queue';

import { Worker } from 'worker_threads'; import path from 'path';

const taskQueue = new TaskQueue(4); // Limit to 4 simultaneous workers function runService(data: any): Promise<any> {

return new Promise((resolve, reject) => {

const worker = new Worker(path.resolve(__dirname, 'worker.ts')); worker.postMessage(data);

worker.on('message', (message) => { resolve(message);

});

worker.on('error', (error) => { reject(error);

});

worker.on('exit', (code) => { if (code !== 0) {

reject(new Error(`Worker stopped with exit code ${code}`));

}

});
```

```
});
}
// Adding tasks to the queue for (let i = 1; i <= 10; i++) {
taskQueue.addTask(() => runService({ value: i }));
}
```
```

By understanding how to create workers and manage tasks efficiently, developers can improve the performance and reliability of their Node.js applications.
```

chapter 11: Testing and Quality Assurance in TypeScript Backend

This chapter aims to provide an overview of testing methodologies, tools, best practices, and strategies for effective quality assurance in a TypeScript-based backend environment.

1. The Importance of Testing

The significance of testing in backend development cannot be overstated. Here are a few key reasons why testing is essential:

Reliability: Rigorous testing ensures that the application behaves as expected, reducing the likelihood of bugs arising in production.

Maintainability: Well-tested codebases are easier to maintain. Tests act as documentation, helping developers understand the intended behavior of the code.

Refactoring Safety: Having a comprehensive suite of tests enables developers to refactor code with confidence, as the tests will help ensure that functionality remains intact.

Improved Collaboration: A robust testing framework facilitates collaboration among team members. New developers can quickly understand the code's purpose and intended behavior through tests.

2. Types of Testing

In the context of TypeScript for backend development, several types of testing can be employed: ### 2.1 Unit Testing

Unit testing focuses on testing individual components or functions in isolation. The goal is to validate that each part of the code performs as expected. Tools like Jest and Mocha are popular choices for writing unit tests in TypeScript.

Example: Here's a simple example using Jest to test a function:

```typescript
// math.ts

export function add(a: number, b: number): number {
return a + b;
}
// math.test.ts

import { add } from './math';

test('adds 1 + 2 to equal 3', () => { expect(add(1, 2)).toBe(3);
});
```

2.2 Integration Testing

Integration tests check how different modules or services work together. In a TypeScript backend, this might involve testing the interactions between different APIs, databases, and other services.

Example: Using Supertest to integrate with an Express server:

```typescript
```

```
import request from 'supertest';

import app from './app'; // Your Express app

describe('GET /api/users', () => {

it('should respond with an array of users', async () => {
const response = await request(app).get('/api/users');
expect(response.status).toBe(200);
expect(Array.isArray(response.body)).toBe(true);

});

});
```
` ` `

2.3 End-to-End Testing

End-to-end (E2E) tests validate the application's flow from start to finish. This testing approach ensures that the entire system is functioning as intended. Frameworks like Cypress or Playwright can be integrated to facilitate E2E testing.

2.4 Performance Testing

Performance testing evaluates the application's behavior under load. Tools like Artillery or JMeter can be utilized to simulate traffic and evaluate response times, throughput, and resource utilization.

3. Testing Tools and Libraries ### 3.1 Jest

Jest is a popular JavaScript testing framework that works seamlessly with TypeScript. With built-in support for mocking, snapshot testing, and coverage reporting, Jest is an excellent choice for unit and integration tests.

3.2 Mocha and Chai

Mocha is a flexible testing framework that can be complemented with Chai for assertion functionality. This combination is commonly used in Node.js applications.

3.3 Supertest

Supertest is a library for testing HTTP servers. It provides a high-level API to simplify writing integration tests for RESTful services.

3.4 TypeORM and Database Testing

When working with databases, frameworks like TypeORM can assist in facilitating testing. In-memory databases such as SQLite can be utilized during tests to avoid polluting production data.

4. Test-Driven Development (TDD)

Test-Driven Development (TDD) is an approach where tests are written before writing the corresponding code. This practice may enhance code quality and design, promoting the development of modular and testable components.

TDD Cycle:

Write a failing test: Determine the requirements and write a test that defines desired functionality.

Write the minimum code: Craft just enough code to make the test pass.

Refactor: Clean up the code while ensuring the tests still pass. ## 5. Continuous Integration and Continuous Deployment (CI/CD)

Integrating testing into a CI/CD pipeline ensures that tests run automatically with each change to the code.

Tools like GitHub Actions, Travis CI, and CircleCI can automate running tests and deploying applications, providing immediate feedback to developers about the health of the codebase.

Example CI/CD Steps:

Push code to a shared repository.

Run automated tests in the CI pipeline.

Deploy to a staging environment if tests pass.

Upon approval, deploy to production. ## 6. Best Practices

6.1 Write Clear and Understandable Tests

Tests should be easy to read and understand. Use descriptive test names and clear assertions to document the expected behavior.

6.2 Aim for Code Coverage but Don't Be Overly Obsessed

While aiming for high code coverage is essential, it should not be the sole metric for quality. Focus on testing critical paths and edge cases.

6.3 Avoid Testing Implementation Details

Tests should focus on the observable behavior of the code rather than its internal implementation. This promotes better encapsulation and flexibility in making changes.

6.4 Maintain Your Tests

Just like production code, tests should be refactored and maintained. Prune obsolete tests and keep the suite relevant and efficient.

By employing various testing strategies, using the right

tools, and adhering to best practices, developers can ensure their applications remain reliable and maintainable. As the complexity of software systems continues to grow, an investment in quality assurance is not only wise but necessary for the long-term success of any project.

Writing Unit and Integration Tests with Jest and Supertest

In this chapter, we will explore how to write unit and integration tests for a TypeScript-based backend application using two powerful tools: Jest and Supertest. Jest is a popular testing framework for JavaScript applications, while Supertest is a library that allows you to test HTTP servers in Node.js. By the end of this chapter, you will have a solid understanding of how to set up and implement tests in your TypeScript projects.

Setting Up Your Environment

Before diving into writing tests, we need to set up our development environment. If you haven't already set up a TypeScript backend project, you can create one using the following steps:

Initialize a New Project:

Open your terminal and run the following commands to create a new directory and initiate a package.json file.

```bash
mkdir my-backend cd my-backend npm init -y
```

Install Dependencies:

Install TypeScript, Jest, Supertest, and other necessary dependencies.

```bash
npm install typescript ts-jest @types/jest @types/supertest supertest express body-parser
```

Initialize TypeScript Configuration:

Create a `tsconfig.json` file in the root of your project.

```bash
npx tsc --init
```

Configure Jest:

Create a Jest configuration file by adding the following script to your `package.json`.

```json
"scripts": {
"test": "jest"
}
```

Then, add a `jest.config.js` file to establish Jest settings.

```javascript
module.exports = { preset: 'ts-jest',
testEnvironment: 'node',
};
```

```
` ` `
```

Now that your environment is set up, we can start building our backend application and writing tests for it. ## Building a Simple Express App

For this chapter, we will build a simple Express application that manages a list of items. Create a file named

`app.ts` and implement the following code:

``` typescript
import express from 'express';

import bodyParser from 'body-parser';

const app = express(); app.use(bodyParser.json());

let items: string[] = [];

// Route to get items app.get('/items', (req, res) => {
res.json(items);

});

// Route to add an item app.post('/items', (req, res) => {
const { item } = req.body;

if (!item) {

return res.status(400).json({ error: 'Item is required' });

}

items.push(item);

res.status(201).json({ message: 'Item added', item });

});

export default app;
```

```
```

This application provides two endpoints: one for retrieving items and another for adding items to a list. ## Writing Unit Tests with Jest

Unit tests aim to verify the functionality of individual components in isolation. We will write unit tests for our Express application in a file named `app.test.ts`.

First, create a new directory named `__tests__` in your project root and add the test file:

```bash
mkdir __tests__
touch __tests__/app.test.ts
```

Add the following code to `app.test.ts`:

```typescript
import request from 'supertest'; import app from '../app';

describe('Item API', () => {

it('should return an empty array when no items exist', async () => { const response = await request(app).get('/items');
expect(response.status).toBe(200);
expect(response.body).toEqual([]);
});

it('should add a new item', async () => { const response = await request(app)
```

```
.post('/items')
.send({ item: 'Sample Item' });


expect(response.status).toBe(201);
expect(response.body.message).toBe('Item          added');
expect(response.body.item).toBe('Sample Item');
});
```

it('should return an error when trying to add an item without content', async () => { const response = await request(app)

```
.post('/items')
.send({});


expect(response.status).toBe(400);
expect(response.body.error).toBe('Item is required');
});
});
```
` ` `

Running Unit Tests

Now that we have written our unit tests, let's run them. Execute the following command in your terminal:

` ` `bash npm test
` ` `

You should see the output indicating that all tests have passed. ## Writing Integration Tests

Integration tests evaluate how different parts of the application work together. While our previous tests were more focused on individual routes, integration tests will check various workflows within the application.

In the same `__tests__` directory, we will add a new test file for integration tests. Create a file named

`app.integration.test.ts`:

```bash
touch __tests__/app.integration.test.ts
```

Add the following code to `app.integration.test.ts`:

```typescript
import request from 'supertest'; import app from '../app';

describe('Item API Integration Tests', () => {

it('should add multiple items and retrieve them', async ()
=> { await request(app)

.post('/items')

.send({ item: 'Item 1' });

await request(app)

.post('/items')

.send({ item: 'Item 2' });

const response = await request(app).get('/items');
expect(response.status).toBe(200);
expect(response.body).toEqual(['Item 1', 'Item 2']);
```

```
});

});
```
` ` `

Running Integration Tests

Just like before, you can run your tests using the command:

` ` `bash npm test

` ` `

You should see the results for both your unit and integration tests, verifying that your application behaves as expected.

We covered the fundamentals of writing unit and integration tests using Jest and Supertest in a TypeScript-based backend application. You learned how to set up your environment, create a simple Express application, and write comprehensive tests that ensure your application is functioning correctly. Testing is vital for maintaining high code quality, and incorporating it into your development workflow will help you catch issues early and build robust, reliable software.

Automated Testing Strategies for a Reliable Backend

Automated testing serves as a backbone for achieving this reliability, particularly in backend systems where various components interact. This chapter aims to provide you with practical and efficient strategies for implementing automated testing for your backend services written in

TypeScript.

Why Automated Testing?

Automated testing is the process of executing predefined tests using software tools. Here are a few reasons why automated testing is indispensable for backend development:

Early Detection of Bugs: Frequent testing allows for the early detection of bugs, which can save time and resources in the long run.

Regression Testing: Automated tests can quickly verify that new changes do not introduce regressions.

Documentation: Well-written tests serve as documentation for the expected behavior of your application.

Continuous Integration/Continuous Deployment (CI/CD): Automated tests are integral to CI/CD pipelines, ensuring that only code that passes all tests is deployed.

Types of Tests

When creating a robust testing strategy, it's essential to understand the different types of tests available: ### Unit Tests

Unit tests focus on individual components or functions in isolation. They validate the smallest testable parts of the application in a controlled environment.

Tools:

Jest: The most popular testing framework for

TypeScript that supports mocking and has a rich API for assertions.

Mocha: A flexible test framework that works well with TypeScript when combined with assertion libraries like Chai.

Sample Implementation:

```typescript
// example.test.ts

import { add } from './example';

describe('Addition Function', () => {

it('should return the correct sum of two numbers', () => {
expect(add(1, 2)).toBe(3);

});

});
```

Integration Tests

Integration tests assess how different modules communicate and work together. These tests help ensure that the various components of your system function correctly when combined.

Tools:

Supertest: A popular library for testing HTTP requests in Node.js applications.

Jest: Again, with its powerful mocking features, it can seamlessly handle integration tests. #### Sample Implementation:

```typescript
// app.test.ts

import request from 'supertest';

import app from './app'; // Your Express app

describe('GET /api/users', () => {

it('should return a list of users', async () => {

const response = await request(app).get('/api/users');
expect(response.status).toBe(200);
expect(response.body).toEqual(expect.arrayContaining([expect.objectContaining({ id:

expect.any(Number) })]));

});

});
```

End-to-End Tests

End-to-end (E2E) tests simulate real-user scenarios and validate the application flows across multiple components.

Tools:

Cypress: While traditionally used for front-end testing, it can test API endpoints as well.

Nightwatch.js: Great for testing web applications, can also handle backend API validations. #### Sample Implementation:

```typescript
// e2e.test.ts
```

```
describe('User Flow', () => {

it('should allow a user to register and login', async () => {

await request(app).post('/api/register').send({ username:
'test', password: 'test123' });

const          loginResponse          =          await
request(app).post('/api/login').send({   username:   'test',
password: 'test123'

});

expect(loginResponse.status).toBe(200);

});

});
```
```

### Performance Tests

Performance testing ensures that your backend can handle
the expected load. This is crucial for applications that
experience high traffic.

#### Tools:

**Artillery**: A modern, powerful, and easy-to-use load
testing toolkit.

**K6**: A developer-centric performance testing tool that
enables writing tests in JavaScript. ## Testing Strategies

### Test-Driven Development (TDD)

In TDD, tests are written before the code itself. This
approach forces developers to write only the necessary
code to pass the tests, often resulting in cleaner, more
focused modules.
```

Behavior-Driven Development (BDD)

BDD focuses on the behavior of the application from the user's perspective. Tests are written in a language that non-developers can understand, making collaboration easier.

Continuous Testing

Incorporating automated tests into your CI/CD pipeline enables continuous testing. Each time code is updated, tests are run automatically to ensure that the application is still functioning correctly.

Best Practices for Automated Testing in TypeScript

Keep Tests Isolated: Ensure that unit tests do not depend on external resources or global state.

Mock Expensive Resources: Use mock servers or libraries like `nock` to simulate API responses in your tests.

Organize Tests Logically: Structure your tests in folders that mirror your source code organization for better navigation and maintenance.

Run Tests Frequently: Integrate your tests into the CI/CD pipeline to catch issues early.

Review and Refactor: Just like production code, review and refactor your test code regularly.

Automated testing is essential for building a reliable backend in TypeScript. By incorporating unit, integration, end-to-end, and performance tests into your development workflow, you enhance the stability and maintainability of your applications.

Conclusion

As we reach the end of our journey through "TypeScript for Backend Development," we hope you've gained valuable insights and practical knowledge to elevate your skills in building robust backend applications using TypeScript, Node.js, and Express.

Throughout this book, we've explored the core concepts of TypeScript and the advantages it brings to backend development—particularly in the realm of type safety, scalability, and maintainability. From setting up your development environment to understanding advanced concepts like middleware, databases, and authentication, we aimed to provide a comprehensive guide that caters to both beginners and seasoned developers looking to enhance their expertise.

The evolution of the JavaScript ecosystem has ushered in modern frameworks and tools that empower developers to create efficient and powerful applications. TypeScript's evolving presence in this landscape enhances not only code quality but also developer experience, making it an invaluable asset for backend development.

As you embark on your own projects, remember that the principles of clean architecture, modular design, and the use of TypeScript's features to their fullest potential will set you apart. Experiment with the examples provided, explore additional libraries, and don't hesitate to dive deeper into the community resources available.

In the ever-evolving world of technology, continuous

learning is essential. Stay updated with the latest advancements in TypeScript, Node.js, and the broader JavaScript ecosystem, as they continue to grow and adapt to new challenges and opportunities. Engage with developer communities, contribute to open-source projects, and share your knowledge with others—collaboration is key in our field.

Thank you for investing your time in this book. We hope it serves as a helpful reference in your journey towards mastering backend development with TypeScript. May your future projects be successful, innovative, and fulfilling!

Happy coding!

Biography

Adrian Miller is a passionate technologist, web development expert, and the visionary mind behind groundbreaking digital solutions. With a deep-rooted love for **TypeScript programming, web development, and cutting-edge web applications**, Adrian has dedicated his career to transforming ideas into dynamic, high-performance digital experiences.

Driven by an insatiable curiosity and a commitment to innovation, Adriam's expertise spans across front-end and back-end development, harnessing the power of modern technologies to build scalable and efficient web applications. His ability to **simplify complex concepts and turn them into actionable insights** makes his work not only powerful but also accessible to developers and entrepreneurs alike.

Beyond coding, Adrian is an advocate for **continuous learning and sharing knowledge**, believing that the digital world thrives when creators push boundaries and explore new possibilities. Whether crafting seamless user interfaces, optimizing performance, or mentoring aspiring developers, his passion for the web shines through in every project he undertakes.

In this book, Adrian distills his **years of experience, practical know-how, and innovative mindset** into a comprehensive guide that empowers readers to **master Miller** and elevate their development skills to new heights. If you're ready to unlock your full potential in web development, you're in the right place—Adrian Miller is here to guide you on the journey.

Glossary: TypeScript for Backend Development

A

API (Application Programming Interface)

A set of rules and protocols for building and interacting with software applications. In the context of backend development, APIs allow different parts of a system to communicate with each other and provide services to clients, such as web and mobile applications.

Async/Await

A syntactic feature in TypeScript (and JavaScript) that allows developers to write asynchronous code in a more synchronous-like style. The `async` keyword is used to declare asynchronous functions, and `await` is used within those functions to pause execution until a Promise resolves.

B

Backend

The server-side of a computer application and everything that communicates between the database and the browser. The backend is responsible for business logic, database interactions, user authentication, and server configuration.

Bcrypt

A popular hashing library used in Node.js that helps securely hash passwords before storing them in a database. It provides methods for generating and comparing hashed passwords, making user authentication safer.

C

Class

A blueprint for creating objects in TypeScript, providing a way to encapsulate data and functionality together. Classes can include properties, methods, and can implement inheritance.

Compiler

A tool that transforms TypeScript code into JavaScript, enabling it to run in environments that support JavaScript, such as Node.js. The TypeScript compiler checks for type errors and other potential issues before the code is executed.

D

Decorators

A TypeScript feature that allows adding metadata to classes, methods, or properties. They are often used in frameworks like Angular and NestJS to enhance functionalities, such as dependency injection.

Dependency Injection

A design pattern used in backend development where a class receives its dependencies from external sources rather than creating them internally. This promotes loose coupling, easier testing, and better code organization.

E

Endpoint

A specific URL or URI within an API where requests can be made to access resources or services. Each endpoint is typically associated with a specific functionality—such as retrieving or updating data.

Express.js

A fast and minimalist web application framework for Node.js, providing robust tools for building web applications and APIs. It streamlines the server-side development process, allowing developers to create routes, manage requests, and integrate middleware easily.

G

Generic Types

A TypeScript feature that enables developers to create reusable components and functions that work with any data type, enhancing code flexibility and type safety.

I

Interface

A TypeScript construct that defines a contract for classes or objects. It specifies the structure and types of properties and methods and serves as a blueprint for implementing consistent data shapes.

Instance

An individual occurrence of a class created with the `new` keyword. Each instance has its own set of properties and methods defined in the class.

J

JSON (JavaScript Object Notation)

A lightweight data interchange format that is easy for humans to read and write and easy for machines to parse and generate. JSON is commonly used for transmitting data between a server and a client in APIs.

M

Middleware

A function or code segment in Express.js and other frameworks that process requests and responses. Middleware can perform tasks such as logging, authentication, and error handling between the request and response phases of application execution.

N

Node.js

A JavaScript runtime built on Chrome's V8 engine that allows developers to execute JavaScript code server-side.

It leverages an event-driven, non-blocking I/O model, making it suitable for building scalable network applications.

P

Promise

A JavaScript object representing the eventual completion or failure of an asynchronous operation and its resulting value. Promises are central to managing asynchronous tasks in TypeScript and JavaScript.

REST (Representational State Transfer)

An architectural style for designing networked applications. It utilizes standard HTTP methods (GET, POST, PUT, DELETE) for communication and is widely used for building web APIs.

T

Type

A TypeScript construct that defines the kinds of values that can be assigned to a variable, function parameters, or return values. Primitive types include `number`, `string`, and `boolean`, while complex types can include `arrays`, `tuples`, and `objects`.

Type Inference

The automatic detection of type by the TypeScript compiler when a variable is initialized, allowing developers to write less code while maintaining type safety.

TypeScript

A typed superset of JavaScript that adds optional static

typing to the language, enabling developers to catch errors at compile time and enhancing the development experience through better tooling and code quality.

U

Universal Type

A concept in TypeScript indicating a type that can accommodate any value. The `unknown` and `any` types allow flexibility but should be used cautiously to maintain type safety.

V

Valgrind

A programming tool used for memory debugging, memory leak detection, and profiling. While not directly related to TypeScript, understanding performance and memory management can be crucial in backend development.

Variables

Named storage locations in programming that hold values which can be changed during execution. TypeScript allows declaring variables with specific types, enhancing code clarity and reducing runtime errors.

W

Wrapper

A design pattern used to create a new interface around an existing code component, often enhancing or simplifying its functionality. This is common in middleware and service integration scenarios.

www.ingramcontent.com/pod-product-compliance
Lightning Source LLC
La Vergne TN
LVHW051322050326
832903LV00031B/3305

* 9 7 9 8 3 0 9 9 9 0 5 1 1 *